CATCH WRESTLING
The Original Submission Art

Guillermo Diaz

DEDICATION

This book is dedicated to Catch Wrestling Instructor

Billy "The Ripper" Warlock

Catch Wrestling: The Original Submission Art
By Guillermo Diaz
Edited by Fernan Vargas
Copyright © 2024 Fernan Vargas

First Printing: 2024
Off the Books, Books
Chicago, Illinois USA 60107

Table of Contents

Foreword

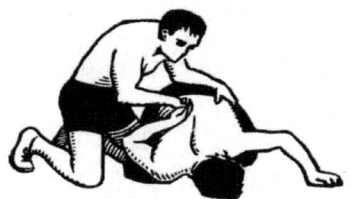

The Legacy, Myth, and Resurrection of a Fighting Art That Never Tapped Out

Catch wrestling was never built for the spotlight. It was born in coal pits and carnivals, where sweat hit canvas under flickering gas lamps and matches ended with bones bent and shoulders pinned. Long before "tap or snap" became a slogan, it was a quiet philosophy whispered between hookers and stretchers: win clean, win quick, and never show your hand unless it's locked around someone's wrist.

The men who carried this art were often forgotten—or worse, absorbed into a circus of sequins and gimmicks. Their holds remained, but the context vanished. Catch became a ghost in the machine of modern wrestling: alive in motion, but invisible in name. Its language—wrist ride, double wrist lock, toe hold, quarter nelson—was whispered in dark gyms, passed down through pain, patience, and precision.

But ghosts don't rest forever.

In recent years, catch-as-catch-can has clawed its way back onto the mats—not as nostalgia, but as a living, breathing system. Fighters, grapplers, and curious thinkers from around the world are rediscovering its brutal clarity. Organizations are forming. Tournaments are growing.

Lineages are being honored. And most importantly, students are sweating, learning, and cranking in its name.

This book is a tribute to the art that wouldn't die. It's for the bruised and the brave, the scholars and the showmen, the ones who know that inside every pin and crank lies a philosophy: of pressure, control, leverage, and grit.

Catch wrestling didn't tap out.
It just waited for the right moment to reverse position.

Introduction:

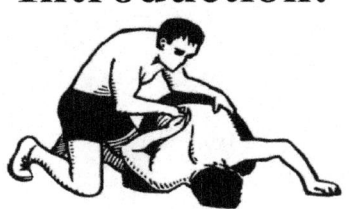

What Is Catch Wrestling (Really)?

Separating hooks from hype in a style that shaped combat sports and never got its due

Catch wrestling isn't folklore. It isn't fake. And it sure as hell isn't forgotten—not by the ones who've felt it.

Before it was co-opted, rebranded, or buried under pyrotechnics and promos, catch-as-catch-can was raw wrestling: unscripted, unforgiving, and unrelentingly effective. Born in the dirt and sweat of 19th-century England, catch was a fusion of folk styles from miners, laborers, and carnival hardmen—a practical blend of pins, cranks, and chokes designed to finish a fight, not impress a crowd. It didn't ask for rules. It asked, *Can you go?*

What makes catch different isn't just what it allows—it's what it demands. A catch wrestler must know how to control pressure, ride hips, apply torque, and inflict pain without giving up position. Submissions aren't options—they're expectations. Hooks aren't flashy gambits—they're calculated endgames. And while modern grappling arts often prioritize positional dominance or point strategy, catch rewards cunning, aggression, and adaptability.

Yet for all its influence, catch wrestling rarely gets the credit it deserves. It seeded the roots of professional wrestling, bled into early MMA through the hands of men like Ken Shamrock and Josh Barnett, and shaped the submission arsenal of many who've never heard its name. Some call it a lost art. Others know it never really left.

This book exists to shine a light on the legacy and living pulse of catch wrestling—not as nostalgia, but as a fighting style with teeth. We'll walk through its blood-and-sawdust origins, trace its journey through circuses and strongholds, and meet the athletes who carry its hooks into rings, cages, and studios today.

Catch wrestling isn't pretty. It's pressure and pain dressed in discipline. And it's long past due for its return to center stage. Let's unroll the canvas and find out what's real

Chapter 1:

Rough & Ready – England's Back-Alley Birthplace

Before catch wrestling was a system, it was a scuffle. It began not in polished gyms or glimmering stadiums, but in the rough corners of industrial England—Lancashire, to be precise. In the 1800s, the textile towns and coal pits of northern England buzzed with working-class energy. Life was hard, and the leisure of the masses was just as rugged. Among the alehouses, county fairs, and cobbled alleys, a style of grappling began to emerge that was raw, fast, and unapologetically real.

Lancashire's Folk Roots

Wrestling had long been a part of English culture—styles like Cumberland and Westmorland wrestling were more traditional and gentlemanly, often with restrictive rules about grips and throws. But in Lancashire, where factory workers and colliers needed an outlet more visceral, a new form took shape: *catch-as-catch-can*. The name said it all— "catch" any hold you can, with little restriction. The only thing that mattered was whether you could control your opponent and finish the fight, either by pinning their shoulders or twisting a joint until they begged off.

What separated Lancashire catch from older folk styles was its emphasis on innovation. Grapplers began experimenting with joint locks, cradles, and clever transitions—anything to give them the edge in a quick, often impromptu scrap. These were matches without mats, often without referees. They happened behind pubs, in fields, or between work shifts when wagers were laid and reputations were on the line.

The Rise of the "Hooks"

Out of this world of muddy boots and brick dust came the early "hookers"—grapplers who mastered the art of submission. They didn't just wrestle to win; they wrestled to dominate. The term "hook" referred to a painful joint lock or submission hold, and a true hooker was both feared and respected. In Lancashire, if you could hook someone, you weren't just tough—you were dangerous.

And yet, despite its brutality, catch wrestling was intelligent. It wasn't just strength but pressure, timing, and cunning that turned the tide. It was often said that one good hooker could beat three strong men—and more than a few pub brawls turned into unexpected clinics.

From Fields to Fairgrounds

As the style matured, wrestlers began taking their skills on the road, performing at county fairs, carnivals, and traveling shows. Matches became spectacles, and challenges to the public were common—"£5 to anyone who can last 10 minutes with the champion." It was part combat, part theater, but the danger was always real.

The sport now had eyes on it—and for the first time, structure began to form. Rules emerged, organizers took interest, and the style continued evolving. But at its heart, catch remained what it had always been: honest, unforgiving wrestling born from the grit of survival.

A Legacy Pinned in Place

The men of Lancashire didn't set out to create a martial art. They were laborers, miners, and fighters looking to prove themselves in a world that didn't offer many second chances. Yet what they built—with little more than bruised knuckles and sheer will—became the backbone of a grappling lineage that would stretch from snake pits to shoot fights to MMA cages around the world.

Catch wrestling wasn't carved out in marble halls. It was dragged, cranked, and pinned into history by men who knew only one thing: never quit, and never give your back.

And that, more than anything, is where the story begins.

Chapter 2:

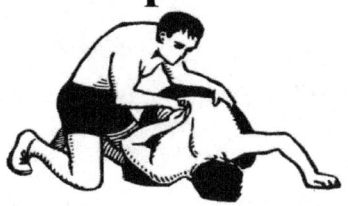

Hold as Catch Can – The Style That Wouldn't Be Tamed

Catch-as-catch-can wasn't built for etiquette—it was built for efficiency. Stripped of ceremonial holds or style-based restrictions, it emerged as a wrestling philosophy that prioritized adaptability, cunning, and control. "Catch" meant exactly that: catch any hold you can, from any position, and do it before your opponent does. And it was this open-ended ethos that transformed catch wrestling from a rough pastime into a technical revolution.

Unlike other grappling styles that emphasized structure— dictated grips, limited ranges of motion, and cultural formalities—catch took a proudly unrefined approach: no prescribed start positions, minimal rules, no uniform. The only goals were clear: pin him, hook him, finish him.

The Birth of the Hooker

In early catch, a "hook" wasn't an abstract concept—it was pain you could feel. The hooker, a specialist in painful and often fight-ending holds, was the cerebral apex predator of the mat. These weren't brute brawlers—they were tacticians. They baited traps, disguised transitions, and snapped on submissions with surgical timing. Toe holds, neck cranks, hammerlocks, and double wrist locks—each one a weapon sharpened by experience, often applied with zero warning.

Catch taught you to think fast and move faster. Mistakes didn't just cost you points—they meant you got pinned or cranked. And because catch often unfolded without time limits or referees, conditioning, strategy, and psychological warfare became as important as grip strength.

The Pressure Philosophy

What separated catch from most other arts was its top-heavy philosophy of constant pressure. If you weren't attacking, you were being attacked. Leg rides weren't just control—they were launching pads. Crossfaces weren't just rough—they were tactical distractions. Every inch gained meant leverage to work a finish, and the best catch wrestlers knew how to turn the smallest advantage into absolute domination.

What developed was a style that didn't rely on aesthetics. There were no points for flair. It was aggressive, ugly, technical, and highly effective—what some called "a thinking man's fistfight." You had to chain ideas together in real time, adjust instinctively, and read the body like a book in motion.

The Cradle of Innovation

The true brilliance of catch wasn't just the hooks—it was the transitions. Sprawling ride systems, slick turnovers, relentless half-nelson chains, and pressure-filled float passes all formed an ecosystem of relentless attack. Techniques weren't practiced in isolation—they were practiced in flow. That flow, that improvisational genius, is what made catch unstoppable in a world full of rule-bound styles.

While other systems rehearsed moves in static drills, catch forced you to think dynamically. In the coal pits and fairgrounds, there was no second try. You caught or you got caught. This urgency forged wrestlers who were part artist, part predator. And that blend—dangerous, unpolished, and brilliant—is what ensured catch-as-catch-can could never be fully tamed.

Because some styles are born in rulebooks. Catch was born in the wild, and it remembers.

Chapter 3:

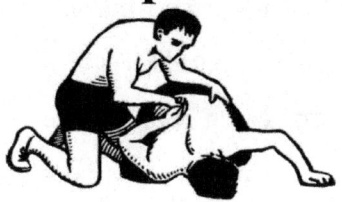

Wrestling, Not Dancing – The Traveling Pros and Prize Ring Shooters

Catch wrestling wasn't meant to stay in the coal towns of Lancashire. Like the men who mastered it, it wandered—looking for work, for wagers, for a crowd. And as the 19th century churned on, catch took to the road, transforming from a roughneck regional style into a traveling spectacle of sweat, skill, and something dangerously close to combat.

The Booth and the Tent

Fairs and carnivals were the perfect launching pad for catch-as-catch-can. Wrestling booths sprang up across England, often as part of larger traveling shows. Inside the canvas enclosures, strongmen issued challenges to the crowd: last five minutes with the champ and win cash or bragging rights. Most matches weren't worked. They were gritty and real—what we'd now call "shoots."

Wrestlers became working pros, living off their winnings and side bets. A journeyman's career was stitched together town by town, match by match. The line between athlete and hustler blurred. There were grapplers who would bait spectators into a match, feign weakness, and then stretch them in humiliating fashion. Others worked together to sell the illusion of chaos, blending real holds with theatrical flair when money and opportunity demanded it.

Prize Rings and Public Blood

In bigger venues—prize rings, music halls, and railway station arenas—wrestling evolved into a staple of working-class entertainment. Promoters emerged. Names like Tom Cannon and Edwin Bibby began gaining recognition. These weren't just tough men—they were skilled technicians who understood pacing, showmanship, and strategy. And when egos or money got involved, the matches got ugly. Submissions were wrenched deeper. Elbows got "accidentally" dropped. Sometimes, it wasn't a match—it was a warning.

The term "shooter" was born here—not just a good wrestler, but a dangerous one. A shooter knew the holds that didn't show well under the lights but left an opponent limping for weeks. If a wrestler got out of line, a shooter was sent in to humble him. Every match had an edge. The crowd might be cheering, but behind the curtain, real grudges simmered.

Catch Goes Global

With industrialization and growing migration, catch didn't stay in England for long. Wrestlers crossed the Atlantic and the Channel, bringing their tools to America, France, and beyond. Some earned fame. Some disappeared in rigged circuits or back-alley brawls. But wherever they went, they taught. They challenged. They fought.

They turned wrestling into a job—and for the lucky few, a legend.

Not a Gentleman's Game

Catch never promised to be clean. It promised to be honest. You won or you didn't. You pinned, or you got pinned. You hooked, or got hooked. In the prize rings, it was wrestling—not dancing. No bows, no points, no protection. Just two men, a canvas, and a crowd waiting to see what would happen when all the rules were optional.

And from that friction, from those bruised ribs and bent wrists, catch-as-catch-can became more than a local tradition. It became a profession. A profession that fought for every inch.

Chapter 4:

Strongmen and Stretchers – Catch Hits the U.S. Carnival Circuit

By the time catch wrestling reached American shores in the late 19th century, it had already earned a rough reputation in England's coalfields and fairgrounds. But in America, it would take on new shape—not by softening, but by adapting. Here, in the land of expanding frontiers and booming industry, catch-as-catch-can found a match made not in heaven, but under canvas: the traveling carnival.

In these dusty showgrounds, surrounded by barkers, oddities, and brass bands, catch didn't just survive—it flourished. It became an act, a spectacle, and for some, a ruthless way of life. America didn't just import the wrestling—it imported the wrestlers: tough, ambitious, and always two steps from either a payday or a broken rib.

Into the Tent

The traveling carnival was the beating heart of American popular entertainment between the 1870s and the 1930s. It brought thrills and wonder to towns too small for theaters, promising everything from snake charmers to feats of strength. Within this swirling tapestry, one of the most visceral attractions was the wrestling tent.

Carnival wrestlers worked behind canvas walls under gaslight, the air thick with sawdust and sweat. The matches weren't slick. They were visceral and immediate. At the center of the show was the "house wrestler," often a legitimate hooker trained in catch techniques who would sit on a raised platform next to the ring, wrapped in towels, staring down anyone brave—or foolish—enough to challenge him.

Step Right Up: The Challenge Match

The central draw was simple but irresistible: "$25 to any man who can last ten minutes with the champ." Local toughs, emboldened by pride or a flask of courage, would climb between the ropes to test themselves. Most lasted less than three. The house wrestler's job was twofold—defeat the challenger, and entertain the crowd doing it. That could mean pinning him decisively, but more often it meant humiliating him.

Sometimes, the match would be competitive—a real "shoot." Other times, the wrestler would toy with the challenger, stretching him slowly with painful holds like neck cranks, toe holds, or wrist locks that didn't break bones but made grown men scream. This wasn't just wrestling. It was theater with bruises.

If the challenger was especially cocky or surprisingly skilled, the gloves came off. The match might devolve into a full-blown submission war. In that moment, the catch wrestler's skills weren't just on display—they were sharpened to a razor's edge.

The Rise of the "Hooker"

This era gave rise to the feared identity of the hooker—not just a wrestler, but a technician who knew how to finish a fight quickly and leave no doubt. While not all house wrestlers were hookers, most were tough, legitimate grapplers with real training. A few rose to legendary status by reputation alone.

The hooker became an insurance policy for the carnival. If any wrestler on the card got out of line, or a match went wrong, the promoter could send in the hooker to stretch someone back into compliance. They were feared even by their colleagues—men who smiled at crowds and shook hands at weigh-ins but carried a deep respect, even fear, of the one guy backstage who could dislocate your shoulder before you realized you were in trouble.

Vaudeville's Velvet Grip

As wrestling gained popularity, it moved into larger circuits—vaudeville theaters, opera houses, and urban sports halls. This brought catch wrestling into contact with more structured entertainment. While the carnival was raw and immediate, vaudeville called for pacing, storytelling, and occasionally, prearranged outcomes.

Slowly, the line between shoot (real) and work (staged) began to blur. Promoters realized that audiences returned not just for the contest but for the drama. Characters were born. Grudges were invented. But beneath the growing gloss, real catch techniques still simmered. A match might be staged in outcome, but the pain was still real.

It was in this crucible of showbiz evolution that modern professional wrestling was born—and it was forged directly from the hooks and holds of catch-as-catch-can.

The Catch of Commerce

Some grapplers refused to compromise their craft. They stayed in the tents, kept their matches real, and their skills honed. Others leaned into the theatrical side of the business. They built personas—The Russian Lion, The Terrible Turk—and drew in crowds by the thousands. Yet even these caricatures were, at their root, products of the carnival environment that catch helped popularize.

Still, for every grappler who made the leap to stardom, dozens more wrestled in obscurity. They broke bones for nickels, traveled in battered boxcars, and stayed one step ahead of being conned or conniving someone else. The traveling circuit was a rough brotherhood—a mash of fraternity, rivalry, and survival.

Behind the Curtain

Promoters controlled the purse strings and the storylines. Wrestlers made money by selling the illusion, but they stayed safe by knowing the real holds. In this backstage world, knowledge was power. Wrestlers who could "go" (legitimately wrestle) earned both respect and better pay. Those who couldn't risked humiliation or injury if a match ever turned real—something that could, and did, happen with little warning.

The phrase "don't shoot on a shooter" wasn't a saying. It was a warning.

Catch Across the Continent

As the carnival spread westward, so did catch wrestling. From the boardwalks of Atlantic City to the muddy lots of Oklahoma, catch left fingerprints in every region. Grappling gyms began to spring up. Fighters brought catch techniques into early boxing matches, barroom brawls, and even the burgeoning world of mixed-style contests.

It wasn't uncommon to see catch wrestlers fight judoka, Greco-Roman specialists, or even boxers in what promoters dubbed "all-styles contests"—prototypes of what we now know as MMA.

The Lasting Grip

Though the carnival circuit would fade, its impact on wrestling is eternal. It was in those grimy tents and gaslit stages that catch became more than a folk tradition. It became a system, a livelihood, and, ultimately, the seed of professional wrestling and submission grappling as we know them today.

The carnival days may be over, but the echoes remain: in the double wrist locks taught in MMA gyms, in the terminology passed down from coach to coach, and in the stories whispered about old hookers who could make men cry with one twist of the hip.

Catch wrestling didn't just entertain America—it toughened it, and in every tent pitched under the stars, another chapter of its legend was written in sweat, silence, and submission.

Chapter 5:

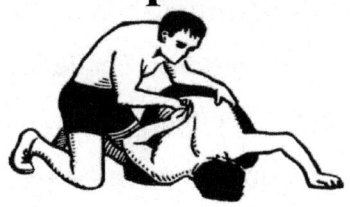

No Rules, Just Results – Catch vs. Everybody

By its very nature, catch wrestling was never content staying in its own lane. It was a style designed to hunt, to adapt, and to dominate—and its practitioners were more than happy to prove that in live, no-nonsense challenge matches against any martial art brave enough to step on the mat. These weren't polite exhibitions or point-based contests. These were raw, rule-bending trials where technique met tenacity, and where the loser didn't just tap—they limped, swallowed pride, or sometimes didn't return at all.

As catch wrestling migrated across borders in the late 19th and early 20th centuries, it began colliding with other established disciplines: the upright formality of Greco-Roman wrestling, the sophisticated throws of Kodokan judo, the fists of boxing, the flowing groundwork of jiu-jitsu. And every time styles clashed, a simple question echoed through gyms, fight halls, and grainy newspaper clippings:

Does your system work when someone's trying to tear it apart?

Breaking Greco's Frame

Greco-Roman wrestling was one of the first established styles to cross paths with catch. Known for its elegant throws and strict ban on leg attacks, Greco was powerful—but rigid. Catch wrestlers capitalized on that, shooting under hips, snagging legs, and tripping with merciless efficiency. In the early 1900s, American catch wrestler Fred Beell shocked European Greco specialists by pinning top champions in under a minute with low attacks and pinning rides they'd never trained to defend.

While Greco's posture and upper-body strength posed real challenges, catch exposed a simple truth: rules that protect a style can also protect its weaknesses. Against catch, there was nowhere safe to stand.

The Santel Shockwave: Catch vs. Kodokan

Nowhere was that lesson learned harder than in Japan, where the Kodokan sent its best judoka to test the rising storm of Western grappling. Enter Ad Santel.

In 1916, Santel—a hard-nosed catch wrestler with a thick neck and a disdain for showmanship—defeated Tokugoro Ito, a 5th-degree black belt from the Kodokan, in front of a stunned San Francisco audience. Santel slammed Ito to the ground and pinned him with brutal control, immediately claiming the title of "World Judo Champion." The Kodokan, wounded in pride and reputation, launched a counteroffensive. More judoka were sent: Daisuke Sakai, Reijiro Nagata, Taro Miyake.

Some of the matches were close. Some ended in draws. But Santel was never broken. His use of pins, neck cranks, and pressure riding overwhelmed the Japanese stylists. These matches left a deep impression. The Kodokan quietly began emphasizing ne-waza—ground fighting—in its curriculum. Santel didn't just beat his opponents. He altered the trajectory of an entire martial tradition.

Puncher Meets Pinner: Catch vs. Boxing

Perhaps no clash drew more visceral attention than wrestler vs. boxer—pure striker versus pure grappler. These matches were kinetic, dangerous, and unpredictable. In one classic encounter, Iowa's Fred Beell was matched against a local boxing favorite under hybrid rules: boxing in round one, wrestling in round two. Beell took a beating in the first but came alive in the second, shooting low and crushing the boxer with a cradle pin that left him breathless and beaten.

But not every wrestler succeeded. Some caught fists before they could close the distance. Others misread timing and were knocked cold. Yet when the wrestler got a grip—on a wrist, a waist, or a leg—it was usually lights out for the puncher.

Tatu and the Birth of Luta Livre

In Brazil, the catch lineage found a new expression through a quiet powerhouse named Euclydes "Tatu" Hatem. Trained in judo and catch wrestling, Tatu became a central figure in the formation of Luta Livre—a Brazilian submission style that emphasized no-gi grappling, leg locks, and real-time violence.

In the early 1940s, Tatu submitted George Gracie—one of the crown jewels of the Gracie family—using a wrist lock straight out of the catch playbook. The Gracies, rooted in Japanese jiu-jitsu, were stunned. Tatu wasn't a showman. He was a pressure-cooker, grinding opponents down with riding control and mean, opportunistic submissions. Later, he would defeat Takeo Yano, a Japanese judoka aligned with the Gracie camp, reinforcing his dominance.

Tatu didn't just win matches. He ignited a rivalry—between gi and no-gi, between prestige and grit, between Luta Livre and Gracie Jiu-Jitsu—that would define decades of Brazilian grappling.

The Zbyszko Enigma

And then there was Wladek Zbyszko—a Polish catch beast with a barrel chest, tree-trunk arms, and a reputation for being unmovable. In 1934, Zbyszko was matched against Helio Gracie, the legendary founder of Gracie Jiu-Jitsu. The bout was billed as epic. Instead, it was subdued—and controversial.

Zbyszko effortlessly controlled Helio, pinning him repeatedly and neutralizing his attacks. Yet, despite dominating, he didn't apply any submissions. Some suggest he was instructed not to "injure the local hero." Others believe he held back intentionally to keep the peace. The match was declared a draw—but almost no one present believed Helio had been his equal.

To catch purists, the match is an open wound—a what-if that hints at the supremacy of old-school hookers kept on a political leash.

Innovation Through Collision

In the end, the challenge matches weren't just clashes. They were crucibles. They forced systems to adapt or ossify. Judo became sharper in ne-waza. Greco practitioners began acknowledging the vulnerability of their rule set. Jiu-jitsu gained ground through refinement—but also faced hard truths about what happens when rules dissolve.

Catch wrestling walked into every one of these encounters uninvited. It wasn't there to win points. It was there to win.

Chapter 6:

Farmer Burns & Frank Gotch – America's First Grappling Icons

Before wrestling was a spectacle, it was a proving ground. And no state in the American Midwest embodied that ethos more fiercely than Iowa—a place where strong backs, harder hands, and relentless work ethic created the perfect storm for wrestling greatness. From this soil rose two of the most formidable names in grappling history: Martin "Farmer" Burns and Frank Gotch. Together, they didn't just dominate the catch wrestling world—they shaped it, elevated it, and forever embedded it into American sporting identity.

The Original Grit: Martin "Farmer" Burns

Born in 1861 in a small Iowa town, Martin Burns grew up doing the kind of work that built real strength—farm labor, lumber hauling, and fence repair. At barely 160 pounds, he looked unassuming. But what Burns lacked in size, he more than made up for in resilience, grip strength, and unmatched technical understanding.

Burns wasn't just a wrestler—he was a thinker, a strategist, and a teacher. Known for his defensive brilliance and legendary neck strength (he could reportedly hang himself from a noose and whistle while suspended), Burns developed a system of grappling that fused old-school toughness with cerebral control. In an era when most matches were still brutal slugfests with little structure, Burns was methodical, studying leverage, holds, and pressure like a scientist in coveralls.

He battled—and beat—the best of his time. He outwrestled heavyweights 50 pounds heavier. His match against Evan "Strangler" Lewis in 1895 made him the recognized American Heavyweight Champion of Catch-As-Catch-Can. That same year, he opened the door to his legacy—not just as a wrestler, but as a mentor—by taking on an eager Iowa teenager named Frank Gotch.

Frank Gotch: Wrestling's First Superstar

Frank Gotch was born to immigrant parents in Humboldt, Iowa, in 1877. He was a natural athlete—strong, fast, and driven. When he met Burns in 1899, he was brimming with potential but still rough around the edges. Under Burns' mentorship, Gotch learned not just the physical mechanics of catch wrestling, but the mental chess behind it.

Gotch refined his game in the rough-and-tumble carnival circuits, facing local challengers in punishing "if you last five minutes, you get paid" matches. He honed his style—gritty, pressure-heavy, and merciless. By the early 1900s, Gotch had developed into something rare: a real shooter with charisma.

His big moment came in 1908, when he faced George Hackenschmidt, the "Russian Lion," in what was arguably the biggest wrestling match in the world at the time. Hackenschmidt was undefeated and revered in Europe for his brute strength and Greco-Roman mastery. But Gotch took him to the mat in front of a raucous Chicago crowd—and systematically broke him down.

Over two brutal hours, Gotch used every weapon in the catch arsenal: face locks, leg rides, grinding top pressure, and hard mat returns. He battered Hackenschmidt psychologically as well, jawing at him, fouling when he could get away with it, and refusing to let the foreign champion breathe. Hackenschmidt quit in frustration.

The rematch in 1911 was even bigger—a sold-out affair at Comiskey Park that drew 30,000 fans and national newspaper coverage. Gotch won again, cementing his place not just as the best catch wrestler alive, but as America's first true wrestling icon.

Burns the Builder, Gotch the Brand

What made their legacy unique wasn't just individual dominance—but the passing of the torch. Burns taught Gotch, but also published mail-order courses, ran wrestling schools, and traveled the country spreading catch techniques. His book, *Lessons in Wrestling and Physical Culture*, is still studied today. He taught not just wrestling holds, but how to breathe, train, live. He made catch wrestling a lifestyle.

Gotch, in turn, brought celebrity to the grind. He appeared in vaudeville. He traveled the country giving demonstrations. Children sent him letters. He was a household name before Babe Ruth, and a better-paid athlete than most boxers. But in the ring, he was still catch to the core.

They were opposites in personality—Burns was humble and methodical, Gotch was brash and media-savvy—but together, they made catch wrestling a legitimate American institution.

The Era Before the Work

In the decades after Gotch's retirement and death in 1917, professional wrestling began evolving into the worked entertainment product we recognize today. But during the Burns-Gotch era, catch wrestling was still real—every match a battle for money, honor, and bodily survival.

They existed in that narrow window of purity, before the pinfalls were planned and the rivalries choreographed. And in that space, they built something that couldn't be faked: legitimacy.

Legacy in the Modern World

Iowa still breathes their spirit. The wrestling rooms in high schools and colleges across the Midwest still echo with their ethic: pressure, endurance, control. Gotch's name graces gyms, streets, and tournaments. Burns' methods are studied by catch coaches around the globe.

Modern athletes like Josh Barnett and Erik Paulson cite them. Organizations like Scientific Wrestling trace lineage back to Burns. You see echoes of their style in MMA fighters who favor wrist control over shrimping, who ride instead of stall, who go for the neck when others would reset.

Burns and Gotch made American catch wrestling a force. They made it dangerous. They made it respected.

And they made sure it would never really die.

Chapter 7:

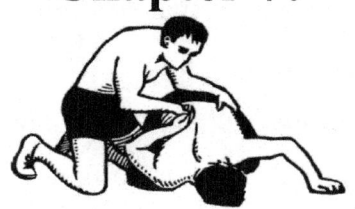

From Hookers to Workers – Catch Goes Hollywood

Before the pyro. Before the promos. Before the crowd learned when to cheer and when to boo—there were men twisting each other on the mat, sometimes for hours, in a brutal, breathless test of pain and pressure. The roots of professional wrestling weren't choreographed. They were contested. And at the heart of that origin story stood the catch wrestler: the shooter, the hooker, the man you didn't challenge for real unless you were willing to leave limping.

But as crowds grew and promoters eyed bigger profits, a transformation began. Catch wrestling didn't just influence pro wrestling—it *became* it. The real began to blur into performance. The shooter learned to work. And the art of grappling crossed the threshold into spectacle.

This chapter is about that evolution—from pain to pageantry, from hook to handshake.

The Hooker's Reputation: Trust and Threat

In the early 1900s, catch wrestling was the gold standard of combat sports. Matches between legends like Frank Gotch and George Hackenschmidt packed arenas and captivated the press. These were long, grueling contests that tested a man's stamina as much as his submission savvy.

But even then, reality had its limits. Audiences loved tension—but they didn't always love a three-hour stalemate. Promoters saw an opportunity: what if the results were planned? What if match length and drama could be controlled, while preserving the illusion of danger?

The key? You still needed real wrestlers—*shooters*—to maintain credibility. That's where the catch hooker came in: both enforcer and insurance policy.

Working the Work: From Shoots to Shows

The shift from shoot matches to "worked" matches didn't happen overnight. It was gradual, often subtle. Some wrestlers began cooperating to deliver more exciting finishes. Others—especially trusted hookers—were brought in to keep things legit... or to "stretch" anyone who went off-script.

Wrestlers like Ad Santel, Farmer Burns, and John Pesek were notorious for being both performers and finishers. They could play the part when needed—and end the game instantly if someone tried to test them. This duality became essential. The worker *had* to be a shooter first.

And with that evolution came vocabulary:

- A **shoot** was a real fight.
- A **work** was a staged contest.
- A **hooker** could do both—and was feared by all.

Promoters like Toots Mondt and Jack Curley helped pioneer the modern pro wrestling format in the 1920s and '30s: predetermined outcomes, time-limited drama, and characters larger than life. But behind every "champion," there was often a quiet catch wrestler keeping the chaos contained.

The Sacred Role of the Enforcer

When a rogue wrestler went off-script—or an outsider tried to break into the business by challenging the locker room— a hooker was called to handle it. These were the "policemen" of the industry.

Guys like Lou Thesz, a true catch stylist, were used to both entertain and to settle things behind closed doors when a message needed sending. In Japan, Karl Gotch played a similar role decades later—training wrestlers to perform, but also ensuring they could *go* if tested.

These men protected the business not by barking, but by *hooking*. Quietly. Effectively. Violently, if required.

Catch Lives in the Work

Even as wrestling evolved into full entertainment, catch's fingerprints remained. The idea of the "submission specialist"? That's a hooker in a different outfit. The chain wrestling in a Zack Sabre Jr. or Bryan Danielson match? That's catch rhythm. The aura of Minoru Suzuki? Pure shooter energy.

And events like *Bloodsport, Pancrase-style rules matches*, and shoot-style wrestling in Japan are modern echoes of the time when the line between real and fake didn't blur—it bent, neck-crank style.

A Legacy Stretched, Not Broken

Catch wrestling may have stepped off center stage when pro wrestling became theater, but it never left the building. It simply took a seat behind the curtain—coaching, enforcing, influencing. And for those who know, there's a moment in every great match where the work drops its mask and the hold *tightens just a little too real.*

That's catch whispering:
"This was never just a show. Not entirely. Not when I'm in the ring."

And the hookers?
They smile backstage, knowing their art lives on—even when it's wearing sequins.

Chapter 8:

Secrets in the Snake Pit – The Gyms That Refused to Forget

As the golden age of American catch wrestling faded into the neon glow of sports entertainment, something unusual happened. The sport's public image withered, but behind the scenes—in locked rooms, windowless gyms, and sweat-soaked basements—its roots dug deeper.

These were not places with signs or slogans. They weren't built to attract crowds. If anything, they warned them away. Inside, pain wasn't accidental; it was instructional. These were the snake pits—the final guardians of a grappling language too sharp for sport, too raw for theater, and too real to be forgotten.

The Crucible of Wigan

The most legendary of them all stood in the unassuming town of Wigan, England. There, nestled behind a row of working-class homes, Billy Riley's gym quietly shaped some of the most feared wrestlers in the world. No glossy branding. No state-of-the-art equipment. Just unrelenting training and a sacred code: survive, learn, and teach only those who earn it.

Riley, himself a former carnival shooter and hooker, built the gym as a place to preserve catch wrestling's purest form—submission grappling that thrived on pressure, cunning, and cruelty. "Hooking" wasn't just an art; it was a responsibility. And to be considered a "hooker" meant something brutal and sacred.

Men like Karl Gotch, Billy Robinson, Roy Wood, and later, Marty Jones and Tommy Heyes honed their craft there. They didn't train for televised matches. They trained to break men who tried to test them. A badge from Wigan meant you carried pain in your fingers and calculation in your eyes.

Billy Robinson: The Reluctant Missionary

One of Riley's most brilliant protégés was Billy Robinson. Rugged, sharp-tongued, and uncompromising, Robinson carried the spirit of the Snake Pit across the world—first dominating in Europe and North America, and later transforming professional wrestling in Japan.

Unlike many who came from real wrestling into showbiz, Robinson never fully softened the edges. He brought real catch into pro wrestling and later MMA. He taught seminars where smiles were rare and correction came with torque. His sessions were legendarily tough: just five minutes drilling a front headlock with him could leave a trained grappler dazed.

Robinson's students include some of the most respected hybrid fighters of the modern era—Josh Barnett, Kazushi Sakuraba, Erik Paulson. He didn't just teach technique. He passed down a lineage. Quietly. Fiercely.

Karl Gotch and the Japanese Resurgence

Another disciple of Riley's gym, Karl Gotch, became an icon in Japan—revered not just for his wrestling acumen, but for introducing a training system that emphasized conditioning, philosophy, and disciplined pain. He brought catch to the Japanese dojos, helping forge the foundations of strong style and shoot-style wrestling.

His influence extended to stars like Antonio Inoki, Akira Maeda, and Nobuhiko Takada—men who blurred the line between legitimate fighting and performance but always trained as if they were preparing for war.

Gotch's sessions were austere, militaristic, steeped in pushups, squats, sprawls, and pain. He didn't speak much. His holds did the talking.

Catch in the Dojo: Sakuraba and the "Gracie Hunter"

Karl Gotch and Billy Robinson's catch teachings filtered into Pancrase, Rings, and eventually Pride Fighting Championships. Out of that ecosystem rose Kazushi Sakuraba—a charismatic, chain-smoking, wildly unorthodox grappler who used leg rides, wrist traps, and neck cranks to dismantle the world's most respected jiu-jitsu dynasty.

Sakuraba didn't just beat Royler, Renzo, and Ryan Gracie—he made it look surgical. Behind his flamboyant persona was a foundation built in real catch wrestling. Leg entanglements, unorthodox pressures, unpredictable rides—he applied Riley's legacy in Tokyo under a barrage of cameras and cheers.

The Hidden American Pits

While Japan revitalized catch wrestling through hybrid competition, the United States preserved it like a relic—quietly, tenderly, in tucked-away places where old shooters kept the flame alive.

Billy Wicks, a feared Southern hooker, taught men how to cripple with a crossface and grind with a top ride. He held no formal school for years, choosing instead to pass knowledge to a handful of devoted pupils. Dick Cardinal, another old-school shooter in Oregon, drilled painful transitions in garages and basements far from the limelight.

These American snake pits weren't trying to "grow the brand." They existed because the coaches couldn't stomach seeing real wrestling lost to time.

Modern-Day Snake Pits

Today, the Snake Pit lives on—some in name, some in philosophy.

Snake Pit U.S.A., founded by Joel Bane, is a structured modern revival that offers formal instruction, certifications, and international camps while preserving the pain-first, pin-focused ethos of catch.

Scientific Wrestling, led by Jake Shannon, curates not only seminars and materials but historical documents, interviews, and archival knowledge from the last generation of hookers.

Other gyms around the world—often buried in MMA academies or judo clubs—embrace catch's blueprint: live grappling, no points, hunt for the hook, feel everything.

What You Learn When You Bleed

To train in a real snake pit is to step away from comfort. It's not about tapping or scoring. It's about enduring. Finding openings in chaos. Applying pressure so relentlessly that it crushes doubt from both bodies.

You don't "get ranked." You get noticed when the old guy stops stretching you and starts showing you things. Catch's oral tradition lives in that moment.

You don't graduate from a snake pit. You become part of it.

The Mat Remembers

When Billy Riley trained his boys in that Wigan shed, he wasn't trying to build champions. He was protecting a language. A way of speaking with the body that could bend a limb or a life if necessary.

That language never died. It's echoed in MMA cages. In no-gi leg entanglements. In drills where you whisper "tighten the ride" and the student groans back.

In every snake pit—in every garage, dojo, and half-lit wrestling room where catch is still practiced—the code remains.

Be quiet.
Be brutal.
Be undeniable.

Because catch wrestling was never meant to be loud. It was meant to survive.

Chapter 9:

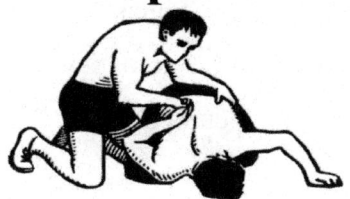

Keepers of the Flame – Gotch, Robinson, and the Wrestling Samurai

While much of the Western world moved on from catch wrestling—burying it under pageantry, pinfall pageants, and performance—two men refused to let it die. They didn't save it through speeches or documentaries. They saved it on the mat.

Karl Gotch and Billy Robinson, both forged in the crucible of Billy Riley's legendary Snake Pit in Wigan, England, didn't just carry the flame of real catch-as-catch-can. They smuggled it across continents and planted it deep in foreign soil. That soil was Japan—and in it, they grew a new kind of warrior: part grappler, part performer, and part samurai.

The Philosopher-King of Pressure: Karl Gotch

Karl Gotch was not flashy. He was not charming. In truth, he scared people. Tall, stoic, and built like a Roman statue with cauliflower ears, Gotch came to Japan not as an entertainer but as a truth-teller. And in a world increasingly focused on spectacle that truth hurt.

Born in Belgium and raised in Germany, Gotch trained in amateur wrestling and Greco-Roman before becoming a disciple of Billy Riley. He absorbed catch wrestling like scripture—favoring riding pressure, submission chains, and an almost spiritual dedication to conditioning.

In Japan, he was revered. The wrestlers there didn't just see him as a visiting trainer. They saw him as a prophet. Antonio Inoki, who would become one of Japan's most iconic pro wrestlers, called Gotch his greatest influence. Others dubbed him "The God of Wrestling."

Gotch's sessions were famously brutal: thousands of squats and Hindu pushups before a single hold was taught. He preached that physical suffering was the path to technical truth. You couldn't fake conditioning. And you couldn't fake mastery.

The Technician With Teeth: Billy Robinson

If Gotch was the philosopher-king, Robinson was the professor in full contact. Sharp-witted, brutally honest, and technically devastating, Robinson took Wigan's painful blueprint and made it global.

Where Gotch was intimidating in silence, Robinson dissected his students aloud—correcting posture, grip, and timing with surgical critique. He wrestled across the UK,

North America, and Japan, gathering titles and scars in equal measure. But it was his role as a coach that echoed loudest.

In Japan, Robinson taught at UWF Snake Pit Japan, overseeing the technical education of a new generation of hybrid fighters. His influence seeped into Pancrase, Rings, and Pride—organizations that shaped early MMA and introduced legions to the unglamorous art of mat control.

Robinson demanded excellence. He didn't teach moves—he taught systems. How to control from the waist ride. How to finish from three-quarters. How to blend submissions like jazz riffs. He didn't care who you were. If your hook was sloppy, he fixed it—with pressure.

Wrestling Meets Bushido: The Evolution of the Wrestling Samurai

What made Japan fertile ground for catch wrestling was its reverence for discipline and lineage. Pro wrestling in Japan—*puroresu*—was always more serious, more physical, and more bound to the martial tradition. In that environment, Gotch and Robinson's methods thrived.

Their students became stars. Antonio Inoki, Yoshiaki Fujiwara, Akira Maeda, Satoru Sayama, Nobuhiko

Takada—each trained in catch principles, each elevated shoot-style wrestling into a new art form. They blended submission wrestling with performance, but never lost the sting of legitimacy.

Wrestlers were no longer just performers. They were *wrestling samurai*—grapplers who trained like warriors and performed like gods.

And when MMA emerged, they were ready. Fighters like Minoru Suzuki and Masakatsu Funaki stepped into real fights with real catch skills. They didn't just survive—they dominated.

The Legacy That Rides

Today, you still see Gotch and Robinson in every Sakuraba scramble, every Josh Barnett neck crank, every time a wrestler ditches the points and rides to break a man's will. Their techniques live on. Their systems are taught in catch academies around the world. Their names are whispered in gyms when a ride gets too tight or a half-nelson turns to pain.

They were never loud about it. They never needed to be. They let the pain speak for them—and it still does.

Chapter 10:

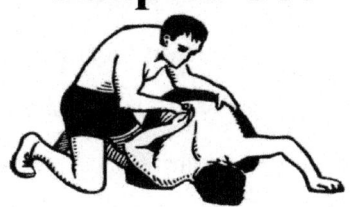

Shoot-Style and the UWF Revolution – Pro Wrestling Reimagined as Real Combat

By the early 1980s, Japanese pro wrestling had reached a crossroads. The pageantry and performance that defined Western wrestling were well established, but a growing segment of fans and fighters craved something more visceral—something that looked like real combat and felt like consequence. They didn't want scripts. They wanted sweat. And at the center of this brewing storm was a quiet but relentless force: catch-as-catch-can wrestling.

Enter the UWF—Universal Wrestling Federation—and the birth of shoot-style wrestling: a genre, a philosophy, a rebellion.

The Rebellion Begins

In 1984, a group of wrestlers broke away from New Japan Pro Wrestling. They were trained, tough, and tired of theatrics. Led by Satoru Sayama (the original Tiger Mask), Akira Maeda, Yoshiaki Fujiwara, and Nobuhiko Takada, these men wanted to make wrestling real again—not by going fully back to shooting, but by creating a new language: the look, intensity, and danger of real fighting, performed with the precision of theater. Catch wrestling provided the grammar.

Their organization—the original UWF—was short-lived but seismic. In it, matches were stripped of flamboyance: no ropes rebounds, no eye pokes, no top-rope moonsaults. Instead, fighters wore kick pads and open-finger gloves. Strikes were stiff. Submissions looked like they could end careers. Holds were drawn directly from the Snake Pit vocabulary—double wrist locks, heel hooks, neck cranks, and brutal ride transitions.

The audience didn't cheer the loudest moment. They held their breath for the smallest twitch—a wrist adjustment, a subtle base shift, a trapped arm.

Catch Wrestling in Every Frame

The heart of shoot-style was unmistakably catch. While judo and karate influenced its outer skin (knees, kicks, throws), the skeleton was pure Lancashire: hooks, rides, and submission over position. Every match played like a live sparring round disguised as theater. Finishers weren't choreography—they were calibrated leverage traps rooted in Billy Robinson's teachings.

Karl Gotch became a mentor to many UWF wrestlers, spreading the same conditioning and mat ethos he taught in the '60s. His fingerprints are on every scramble. Every crossface grip. Every transition that looks like it could've come from an Iowa cornfield or a Wigan coal pit.

Billy Robinson later trained UWF alumni and brought an even sharper edge—coaching future stars like Kazushi Sakuraba and encouraging the bridge between shoot-style and real MMA.

Icons of the Movement

Nobuhiko Takada: Charismatic and dangerous, he blended submission wrestling with legitimate striking, later becoming a symbol of crossover credibility in PRIDE FC.

Yoshiaki Fujiwara: A legitimate catch wrestler and student of Karl Gotch, Fujiwara helped cement shoot-style's technical integrity through UWF and later Fujiwara Gumi.

Akira Maeda: The enforcer. Known for stiff strikes and an intense presence, Maeda's influence helped carry the shoot-style aesthetic into Rings, one of MMA's early proving grounds.

Satoru Sayama: Though famous for his high-flying Tiger Mask persona, Sayama's martial arts leanings led him to create Shooto—a sport built on the backbone of catch and striking hybrids.

These men didn't blur the line between real and fake. They stepped right over it.

A Lasting Impact

UWF folded, reformed, splintered, and birthed new promotions—UWF International, Pro Wrestling Fujiwara Gumi, Rings, and eventually PRIDE. Each new branch took shoot-style into different arenas: more sport-like, more theatrical, or fully combative. Yet in every iteration, the principles of catch endured: control, submission, aggression, and danger.

Even modern Japanese wrestling owes much to UWF. Promotions like Pro Wrestling NOAH and NJPW's "Strong Style" still nod to the stiffness and structure UWF introduced.

And in MMA? The wrist rides, floating pressure, and chain submissions taught in catch have become foundational skills—first introduced to the octagon via Sakuraba and Shamrock, but now common in gyms around the globe.

Shoot-style wasn't nostalgia. It was innovation. It was catch wrestling put on stage without compromise.

And it changed the fight game forever—not by imitating real combat, but by reminding the world what real wrestling looked like when it didn't care about being liked. Only about being undeniable.

Chapter 11:

Pancrase to PRIDE – Catch in the Birth of MMA

Before the world had the UFC, there was Pancrase. Before PRIDE filled Tokyo Domes with thunderous crowds and highlight-reel knockouts, there were gym battles in Japan where the rules were barely written—and the only real law was what worked when things got real. In that undefined space between performance and pure combat, a familiar presence lurked under every sprawl, ride, and neck crank: catch wrestling.

This chapter traces catch's evolution from shoot-style wrestling to true no-nonsense fighting, through the pioneering promotions that brought hybrid grappling to life—and launched the careers of MMA legends who knew how to hook for real.

Pancrase: Where Hooks Hit First

Founded in 1993 by Masakatsu Funaki and Minoru Suzuki—both heavily influenced by Karl Gotch and the UWF movement—Pancrase was designed to be the logical extension of shoot-style wrestling. Strikes were open-hand (at first), submissions were real, and wins came by knockout or tap-out. The result? A proto-MMA organization fueled by pressure, performance, and pain.

Catch wrestling was everywhere: leg rides, face cranks, wrist traps, sprawls into chokes. Fights moved fast, unpredictably, and finished quickly—often with submissions that had fans scrambling to understand what they'd just seen.

Ken Shamrock: The American Hooker Abroad

Trained by Funaki and Suzuki, Ken Shamrock became the bridge between Pancrase and the rest of the world. A raw, powerful athlete with relentless top pressure and a deep submission arsenal, Shamrock turned catch into chaos. His battles with Suzuki, Bas Rutten, and later Royce Gracie in the early UFC cemented him as one of MMA's first crossover stars—and one of catch wrestling's fiercest modern representatives.

He didn't point-fight. He didn't dance. He pinned, smashed, and cranked. His double wrist lock became a staple. His rides were relentless. His reputation: "if Ken gets on top of you, you're not getting back up."

Bas Rutten: The Hooker with Hands

Though Rutten entered Pancrase as a striker, his evolution into a hybrid grappler is one of the sport's greatest case studies. Early losses (to catch-trained wrestlers like Funaki and Shamrock) forced him to dig into submission wrestling. The result? A Dutch striker who became a deadly submission artist—with a catch twist.

He mastered knee bars, heel hooks, and liver shots in equal measure. His later wins in Pancrase and the UFC were built on the catch principles he absorbed through trial, pain, and precision. Rutten would later say catch wrestling changed how he saw fighting: *"If I hit someone and they stay standing, I know I can take them down and finish the job."*

The DNA of PRIDE

PRIDE Fighting Championships, launched in 1997, took the DNA of Pancrase and UWF and infused it with pageantry, high production, and a massive global audience. Its stars— Kazushi Sakuraba, Josh Barnett, Hidehiko Yoshida—often came from catch backgrounds or trained under its lineage.

- **Sakuraba**, the "Gracie Hunter," learned under Billy Robinson and used wrist traps, float passes, and head control to dismantle jiu-jitsu royalty.
- **Josh Barnett**, trained by Erik Paulson and Robinson himself, brought Wigan's fire into the PRIDE ring and later into high-level grappling.

- **Minoru Suzuki**, a Pancrase founder, mixed pain and poetry—always a threat to crank a neck or scoop a leg for a devastating toe hold.

In PRIDE, you didn't win by holding on. You won by putting on a show—and finishing the fight. Catch wrestling, long a ghost in the grappling machine, became the invisible engine behind many of its greatest moments.

Catch in the Cage

By the 2000s, MMA had evolved. Gloves were tighter. Rounds were timed. But catch wrestling's impact hadn't faded—it had simply embedded itself deeper into the art of fighting:

- Pressure rides used to stall and strike.
- Submissions chained from unconventional angles.
- Hooks that weren't just submissions—but statements.

And to this day, when a modern fighter cranks a double wrist lock, floats from mount to cross-body with patience, or traps a leg to ride and suffocate—he's speaking the old language. The one taught in Wigan, whispered in Japan, and shouted into the ring in Pancrase.

Catch wrestling didn't just contribute to MMA—it helped birth it.

From the cage to the canvas, from hooks to high kicks, its presence remains: silent, sharp, and waiting for its next opportunity to finish.

Chapter 12:

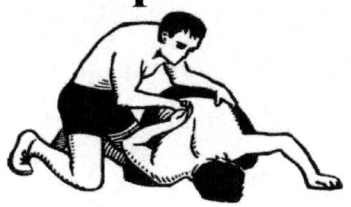

Lessons from the Dojo – The Quiet Teaching of Billy Robinson

By the time Billy Robinson arrived in Japan as a coach, his resume could've filled the walls of a wrestling hall: Snake Pit pedigree, global championships, punishing pro matches, and a bruising reputation that whispered one thing—don't try him for real. But Robinson didn't come to Japan to fight. He came to teach.

And on those quiet mats, barefoot and unsmiling, he did more than instruct. He passed down an entire philosophy— catch wrestling sharpened to its purest edge. What followed wasn't a revival. It was a refinement.

The Dojo Becomes a Lab

Robinson began coaching formally in Japan in the early 2000s, though his influence ran deeper, dating back to the UWF and New Japan's strong style in the '80s. When he officially joined UWF Snake Pit Japan as head instructor, he wasn't interested in fluff, flair, or friendly handshakes. He wanted to rebuild catch from the mat up, one hook at a time.

Sessions started with conditioning that broke the unprepared. Then came drilling—waist rides into knee hooks, floats into arm bars, and the dreaded double wrist lock from every conceivable position. You didn't learn with a curriculum. You learned by being caught.

Robinson would walk among pairs mid-spar, pausing only to growl corrections or demonstrate on the fly—tightening a grip here, torquing a wrist there. Pain was instruction. Tap, reset, repeat.

The Method in the Torture

What set Robinson apart was his relentless focus on detail. A millimeter off on a grip? You'd know when the crank didn't work. Hips a little too high on a ride? You'd eat an escape. He didn't believe in drilling for time. He believed in drilling for truth.

Key elements of his approach included:

- **Pressure first, position second**: Make your opponent suffer just by existing beneath you.
- **Hooks aren't finishes—they're threats**: Each submission sets up the next.
- **The float game**: Weight distribution mattered more than strength. He taught riding like chess—one piece ahead, always.

And above all: *"You're not wrestling to win. You're wrestling to not lose. Everything comes from control."*

The Quiet Legacy

What's striking is how Robinson's teachings filtered into modern MMA without ever being loudly branded. He trained Kazushi Sakuraba, who famously dismantled jiu-jitsu royalty using catch's chaos logic. He sharpened Josh Barnett's ride-heavy, suffocating style. He passed techniques to Erik Paulson, who in turn passed them on to generations of hybrid grapplers worldwide.

Robinson didn't build an empire. He built warriors—one grind, one pressure pass, one crank at a time.

Inside a Robinson Dojo Session

A typical day might look like this:

- **Warm-Up**: 500 Hindu squats, neck bridges, shadow wrestling
- **Drills**: 15 minutes double wrist lock chains, 15 minutes toe hold setups from leg ride
- **Positional Rounds**: Shark tank from front headlock, 1-minute intervals

- **Catch Rounds**: No points, no time—just pressure and pursuit
- **Correction**: "You're high," "You gave space," "Tighter," followed by a slow demonstration—with pain

He didn't yell. He'd fix your mistake by applying it to you. Then you'd never forget.

The Hooker's Echo

In Japan, Robinson's catch was treated like a scroll—not flashy, but sacred. And though he's gone, his teachings remain. They live in dojos across Tokyo and Osaka. They live in Sakuraba's smile when he floats into a wrist trap. They live in Barnett's calm in mount. They live every time a grappler rides rather than resets.

Billy Robinson didn't make catch evolve. He reminded it what it really was.

Control. Pain. Precision. Passed on, not spoken aloud, but whispered on the mat.

Chapter 13:

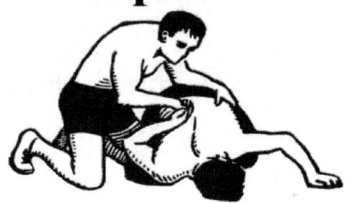

Underground Revival – Catch Crawls Back into the Light

By the turn of the millennium, catch wrestling existed like a ghost in the martial arts world—whispered about, occasionally glimpsed in the hooks of MMA legends, but largely buried beneath the commercial weight of Brazilian jiu-jitsu, judo, and submission wrestling tournaments. Yet the flame never went out. In locker rooms, basements, and off-the-record gym battles, catch wrestling refused to die. And around the 2000s, something unexpected began to stir: a rebirth.

This wasn't a mainstream movement. There were no glossy magazines touting it. No Olympic funding. What revived catch wrestling was hunger—a desire for something older, rougher, and more direct. A style that didn't depend on points or preference but lived in the pain of pressure, pins, and perfectly timed cranks.

The Craving for Roots

As MMA exploded globally, many practitioners began to look backward. They asked: Where did these techniques come from? Why do some transitions feel cleaner? How did early legends like Sakuraba, Shamrock, and Barnett control and submit opponents in ways that didn't align with standard BJJ theory?

The answer kept pointing back to catch wrestling—a system that favored pace over posture, hooks over hierarchy, and leverage over lapels.

This curiosity sparked a wave of fighters, coaches, and hybrid grapplers to seek out the remnants of the art. They didn't find governing bodies or tour buses. They found old men with thick accents and thicker hands, mats that smelled of liniment and rust, and notebooks filled with crude diagrams of neck cranks and figure-four rides.

The revival had begun. Quietly. Violently.

Scientific Wrestling and the Return of the Hook

At the center of this resurgence was Jake Shannon, a relentless historian, athlete, and promoter who founded *Scientific Wrestling* in the early 2000s. Shannon reached out to surviving catch legends like Billy Robinson, Dick Cardinal, Billy Wicks, and Roy Wood, organizing seminars, publishing materials, and building bridges between generations.

Robinson, especially, became the nucleus. Through camps and clinics held across the U.S., Europe, and Japan, he taught a new breed of fighters the forgotten fundamentals—riding pressure, float mechanics, and the art of putting someone down and *keeping them there*. Scientific Wrestling became a clearinghouse for catch curriculum, helping define structure in a style long known for chaos.

The Rise of Catch-Driven Hybrids

While formal catch tournaments were still rare, the revival took root in MMA gyms and submission schools. Fighters began cross-training. Jiu-jitsu practitioners borrowed catch principles—pinning from top, wrist traps, painful crossfaces—to sharpen their game.

The results were felt most in sparring rooms: gi players frustrated by endless pressure. Wrestlers discovering how a little pain could open a lot of space. BJJ brown belts tapping to holds they'd never seen before.

No-gi submission events like *Grapplers Quest* and *ADCC trials* became testing grounds. Catch-trained athletes didn't always win—but they always left an impression. Often literally.

Secret Camps and the Underground Circuit

In Tennessee, Billy Wicks ran "invite-only" intensives for those serious enough to endure catch's grueling pedagogy. In rural Oregon, Dick Cardinal passed on pinning systems and stretching sequences rarely written down. These weren't schools—they were sanctuaries. You learned by getting twisted, held, and taught in real time.

Meanwhile, newer catch coaches like Josh Barnett, Erik Paulson, and Wade Schalles began fusing catch fundamentals with modern training systems. In their hands, catch didn't feel like an ancient art—it felt like the future.

Modern War Rooms

By the 2010s, more gyms were offering catch-inflected classes: in L.A., New York, Denver, Tokyo. Schools affiliated with *Snake Pit U.S.A.* or *Scientific Wrestling* taught structured curriculum—combining historical reverence with real-world adaptation. Drills for wrist rides and cross-body rides joined sprawl drills and leg entanglements.

Suddenly, seminars that used to draw six people in a garage were filling mats with black belts from other systems—eager to explore an art that offered not just technique, but philosophy.

The Internet Hooked In

Podcasts, blogs, and early YouTube clips helped spread catch's gospel. Footage of Billy Robinson crank-demoing seminar students went viral in niche circles. Old matches of Frank Gotch and Karl Gotch were reanalyzed. Grappling nerds dove into match footage, dissecting Sakuraba's traps or Barnett's smothering rides frame by frame.

Where once the snake pit was silent, now its hiss could be heard worldwide.

A Style Still Fighting for a Stage

Despite the growing reverence, catch wrestling remains elusive in modern sport formats. Few events cater exclusively to it. Rule unification is sparse. Tournaments are infrequent, often regional, and sometimes overshadowed by more mainstream grappling events. But that, in a way, keeps catch honest. It's not trendy. It doesn't bend to popularity.

Catch crawled back into the light not because someone sold it, but because enough people still *needed* it.

Needed its grit.

Needed its pain.

Needed the truth it tells—one hook at a time.

Chapter 14:

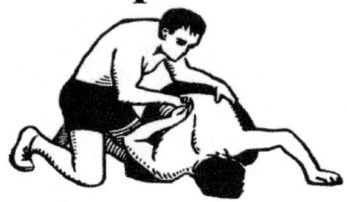

Scientific Wrestling – Codifying a Savage Science

Catch wrestling, long preserved through handshakes, sweat, and scar tissue, has rarely been given the comfort of formal structure. For most of its history, it thrived as an oral tradition—taught by pain, passed through pressure, and guarded by those who knew its secrets not from reading, but from riding. But in the 21st century, a movement began to emerge: not to tame catch wrestling, but to codify it—to shape its curriculum, share its lineage, and give it the legitimacy it has long been denied.

That movement? Scientific Wrestling.

Defining the Undocumented

Scientific Wrestling, founded by Jake Shannon in the early 2000s, was more than a brand—it was a reclamation. Shannon, both an historian and grappler, saw the risk: that catch wrestling's greatest knowledge might disappear with its aging masters. His mission was urgent and ambitious— archive the old ways, honor the lineage, and teach it to those with the grit to carry it forward.

Drawing from the teachings of Billy Wicks, Dick Cardinal, Billy Robinson, Roy Wood, and other torchbearers, Shannon and his team helped give catch a curriculum—not a rigid one, but one that reflected its essence: functional, adaptable, and unrelenting. This wasn't about sport-friendly evolution. It was about making sure the hook still hooked.

Bringing Structure to Pressure

Scientific Wrestling's coaching system and certifications don't reduce catch to sterile techniques. Instead, they focus on:

Foundational Control – pinning systems from the waist ride, cross-body, and spiral.

Submission Chains – multiple finishes from core positions like front headlock, leg ride, and side mount.

Takedown Integration – adapting catch entries into freestyle, folkstyle, and no-gi grappling.

Coaching Psychology – how to teach pain without cruelty; how to maintain the sting without losing safety.

Robinson himself helped shape many of these structures before his death in 2014. His phrase lives on like gospel: *"Learn to control before you submit. Learn to submit before you hurt."*

Bridging Lineages, Building Community

Scientific Wrestling doesn't operate in isolation. It connects with other organizations to strengthen catch's roots:

Snake Pit U.S.A., a system built around the Wigan school, offers a belt-rank progression, global seminars, and competition coaching while preserving no-gi, pin-and-submission-only tenets.

World Catch Wrestling Federation (WCWF) has helped host world championship events with standardized rules.

Catch Wrestling Alliance, founded by Raul Ramirez, promotes international tournaments and blends academic history with live competition.

American Hook Wrestling Alliance (AHWA) brings a more grassroots, club-level energy, welcoming cross-training athletes and new-age grapplers hungry for catch's edge.

Together, these movements support the art from all angles: technical, historical, competitive, and cultural.

Rules Without Rigidity

One of the challenges for catch's modernization is unifying a competitive rule set. Scientific Wrestling's competition blueprint emphasizes:

- **Pinfalls and submissions only**
- **No points, no advantages, no decision wins**
- **Hooks over positions** – the control that leads to damage, not just dominance

In contrast to BJJ, there's no guard pulling. In contrast to amateur wrestling, the goal isn't just to hold—but to hurt.

By preserving this raw format while codifying safety and structure, Scientific Wrestling has helped restore catch's bones without bleaching its soul.

Modern Catchmen and Women

Thanks in part to these efforts, a new generation now trains catch seriously. Athletes cross-training in no-gi, MMA, judo, and wrestling now seek out catch camps. Instructors like Curran Jacobs, Kris Iatskevich, and Joel Bane continue to refine and teach the art internationally. Clinics from the U.S. to Poland to Brazil feature young hookers learning how to apply a crossface like a weapon and ride like they mean it.

And thanks to open-source systems like Scientific Wrestling's *Assistant Coach Program* and the *Certified Catch Wrestler* track, knowledge that was once trapped in a gym in Wigan now travels the globe—under watchful, experienced guidance.

Saving the Savage Without Sanding the Edges

Catch wrestling was born from chaos. But that doesn't mean it has to stay buried in it. Scientific Wrestling and its fellow federations aren't trying to polish catch into something pretty. They're preserving its sharpness and sharing its grip.

In gyms, camps, and underground mats around the world, catch isn't just practiced—it's protected.

Not tamed.
Not diluted.
But understood.

One crank at a time.

Chapter 15:

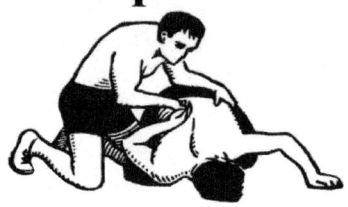

Hooks in the Octagon – Catch in Modern MMA

Modern MMA moves fast. Fakes, fakes, feints. A flurry on the feet, a change in level, a clinch at the fence—then down they go. The crowd watches for knockouts, for chokes, for blood. But what they rarely see—what even seasoned analysts sometimes miss—is the pressure.

The ride. The float. The moment a wrist disappears and a leg is trapped and the fighter on top isn't just holding—they're hunting.

That's where catch wrestling lives: not in highlight-reel moments, but in the inches between control and collapse. This chapter is for those fighters. The ones who bring hooks into the cage and leave their mark without saying a word.

The Style That Never Left

Catch wrestling never declared itself in MMA. It didn't trademark its techniques or build flashy camps. It just showed up—in the way certain fighters held position a little longer, or set up their submissions with gritty, unspectacular transitions that worked *every* time.

Even the term "catch wrestler" rarely appears on broadcast graphics. Instead, fans might hear "submission grappler," "freestyle base," or "dirty top game." But scratch the surface, and you'll find the fingerprints of Wigan and Billy Robinson smeared across decades of cage fighting.

The Masters of Pressure

Some fighters didn't just bring catch into MMA—they embodied it.

Josh Barnett

A heavyweight in size, a technician in spirit, Barnett trained under Erik Paulson and directly with Billy Robinson. He fused catch pressure with sambo leg attacks and judo grips. His ride control was relentless, and his ability to float from mount to submission made his top game suffocating. Whether in PRIDE or the UFC, Barnett showed that pinning could still break men—even when striking was allowed.

Kazushi Sakuraba

Japan's "Gracie Hunter" learned under Robinson and adapted catch's unpredictability into a style entirely his own. He didn't always win, but he always *fought*. His use of wrist traps, misdirection, and unorthodox top control made him a fan favorite—and a catch legend in everything but name.

Erik Paulson

Though better known as a coach, Paulson blended shoot-style wrestling, catch principles, and striking into a hybrid system that produced versatile fighters like Sean Sherk and Josh Barnett. His curriculum includes toe holds, leg rides, neck cranks—the pain, polished and modernized.

Catch in Disguise

Even fighters without formal catch lineage use its tools:

Khabib Nurmagomedov's wrist rides, seated floats, and half-nelson traps from top look very much like catch taught in the Snake Pit.

Randy Couture's dirty boxing from the clinch and grinding mat control echoed carnival roughness.

Tony Ferguson, in his chaos, uses traditional wrestling rides into slicer submissions, head-and-arm traps, and sneaky shoulder pressure—all vintage catch material.

Valentina Shevchenko's transitions from control to finish (especially from mount) contain eerie similarities to catch pin-to-crank sequences—perhaps drawn from sambo, perhaps a natural convergence.

Catch's spirit shows up not because it's taught directly—but because it works.

The Modern Mat Storm

Today's MMA landscape sees catch adapted and fused everywhere:

- Fighters drill *float drills* instead of just positional passes
- Pressure is seen not as stalling, but as *offense*
- Ride time and "wrestling-with-subs" has replaced the old jiu-jitsu vs. wrestling binary

Prominent modern coaches like Firas Zahabi, Danaher, and Barnett all praise catch's brutal efficiency—especially its transitions and philosophy: don't wait for the tap. Take it.

The Invisible Influence

No fighter yells, "Here comes the toe hold from Wigan!" when they attack the ankle. No commentator says, "This front headlock float is straight from Frank Gotch's playbook." But that's what makes catch special. It's *everywhere*—quietly. Effectively.

In every gym where fighters learn to ride instead of reset, control before they submit, or punish transitions with purpose, catch is winning.

It doesn't need a belt. It doesn't need a gi.
It just needs pressure, precision… and one good hook.

Chapter 16:

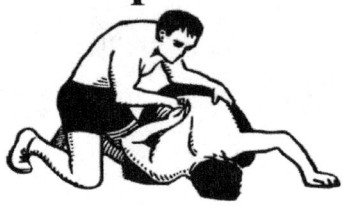

Rufino dos Santos, Euclydes "Tatu" Hatem, and the hidden legacy of catch grappling in Brazil

This book focuses on the global story of **catch wrestling**— its origins, evolution, and modern-day revival. Among its most compelling branches is the quietly revolutionary lineage that took hold in Brazil, where catch's aggressive, submission-first philosophy formed the blueprint of **Luta Livre**, a no-gi grappling art that repeatedly challenged the dominance of Brazilian jiu-jitsu. At the heart of this untold story are two figures who made catch wrestling more than an imported curiosity—they turned it into a national force. Their names are **Rufino dos Santos** and **Euclydes "Tatu" Hatem**.

Rufino dos Santos: Catch's Unseen Apostle in Brazil

Rufino dos Santos's journey began in 1900 in relative obscurity. As a teenager seeking escape from poverty, he stowed away on a ship bound for New York. With no money, no language, and no guide but his own will, he entered a world unknown to him. Yet it was there—inside a YMCA gym—that he encountered **catch-as-catch-can wrestling**: a raw, brutal, submission-based system grounded in leverage, control, and efficient finishing. Rufino was captivated.

Over the next decade, he tested himself in over fifty documented matches across America and Europe— competing in the U.S. and abroad, even during his time in the U.S. Navy. Each bout sharpened his understanding of pressure wrestling. He became known for his mastery of position and painful submission holds, traits that would later define Luta Livre.

Back in Brazil, Rufino took on a humble role teaching physical education and promoting catch-style wrestling in the Navy and YMCA. Though his influence was largely behind the scenes, his greatest impact would come during a challenge match in 1931. During a Gracie-Jiu-Jitsu exhibition held at Rio's Fluminense Stadium, **Carlos Gracie**—-fresh off a series of public victories—boasted he could beat any man in under three minutes. Apparently unmoved, Rufino donned the ring, unbuttoned his coat, and issued a direct challenge.

What followed was a landmark moment. The rematch between Rufino and Carlos turned into a masterclass in catch wrestling technique. Utilizing **relentless shoulder pressure, body control, and timed submissions**, Rufino repeatedly forced Carlos into defensive escape attempts. Eventually, the combination of dominance and fatigue led to Carlos forfeiting the match. Rufino's victory wasn't just a personal triumph—it was a statement: catch wrestling had come to Brazil, and it could defeat even jiu-jitsu's most public legend.

Rufino's victory, however, had a cost. In 1932, after publishing a public letter calling out Gracie refusals to match him, he was ambushed by **Carlos, Hélio, and George Gracie**—allegedly struck with metal tools and subjected to a dislocated arm lock that ended his competitive career. Though the attackers were briefly charged and imprisoned, the episode was a stark reminder of the risks inherent in challenging jiu-jitsu's emerging empire. Rufino faded from public view, but the seeds of catch wrestling had already been planted in Brazilian soil.

Euclydes "Tatu" Hatem: Catch's Champion in Action

Two generations later, Euclydes "Tatu" Hatem solidified catch wrestling's legacy in Brazil. Born in 1914 in Rio, Tatu began his martial journey in Greco-Roman wrestling, but it was catch wrestling's submission-oriented approach that resonated most deeply. Combining jaw-cranking cranks, painful wrist locks, relentless top pressure, and relentless positional dominance, Tatu shaped what became Luta Livre

Esportiva—a raw, no-gi grappling system built not for ceremony, but for combat.

Between the 1930s and the 1950s, Tatu made Brazil watch catch wrestling live in action. His key victories include:

Against George Gracie (1940): In a high-profile no-gi match, Tatu submitted George Gracie—the widely respected jiu-jitsu fighter—using a **rear-naked choke in the second round**. This wasn't a ceremonial hold; it was a forced tapout rooted in catch principles. The match fractured the myth of the Gracie invincibility, proving that Luta Livre, catch's direct descendant, could deliver results in no uncertain terms.

Charles Ulsemer: The French wrestling champion first drew with Tatu, but in a follow-up match, Tatu applied **crank-and-isolate pressure**, forcing Ulsemer to submit. His ability to adjust and implement catch-based pressure showed that Luta Livre wasn't merely reactive—it was evolving its own methodology.

Takeo Yano: The skilled Japanese judoka had impressed with structured groundwork, but Tatu took their final match through a **combination of top control and submission**

entries—a catch wrestling approach that spoke volumes when the submission came.

Leon "Mountain Man" Falkenstein: Tatu's victory over Falkenstein—a Russian superheavyweight—came in a staggering **37 seconds**, twice. Tatu's technique allowed him to penetrate a much larger opponent's defenses, execute takedowns, and apply submissions, proving catch's engineering could overcome size.

Valdemar Santana: Even after stepping back from active competition, Tatu faced Santana—a powerful fighter who later defeated Hélio Gracie—and **subdued him swiftly and decisively** at his own gym. Age and ringside wear had not dulled catch's edge.

Two Stories, One Thread

Rufino dos Santos and Euclydes "Tatu" Hatem represent two distinct chapters in the narrative of catch wrestling's transplantation to Brazil. Rufino, an outsider who studied and fought catch abroad before returning home; Tatu, a native son who forged a Brazilian expression of catch grappling. Each man delivered a jiu-jitsu-era Gracie submission—a direct challenge to jiu-jitsu's claim as the undisputed Brazilian grappling art.

Their overlapping philosophies highlight a continuation: pressure-first control, pain-inspiring submissions, ride-and-isolate tactics, and above all, relentless offense. Their achievements show catch wrestling was not just an imported novelty—it was a method that could be refined and embedded in Brazil's cultural landscape.

Catch Legacy in Modern MMA

Today, the resonances of Rufino's and Tatu's accomplishments can still be felt around the world:

Heel hooks and **kimuras** becoming staples in MMA and no-gi grappling.

Positional top pressure borrowed from catch is taught at camps worldwide.

Wrist cranks, neck locks, and **submission-first thinking**—these are core to grappling approaches influenced by catch wrestling, not jiu-jitsu.

While jiu-jitsu's gi-based popularity skyrocketed, catch-influenced styles quietly shaped MMA grappling from the ground up.

Catch's Quiet Triumph

This chapter shows that catch wrestling was more than a passing curiosity in Brazil—it was a seed of covert revolution. Rufino dos Santos challenged jiu-jitsu's foundations with catch principles before disappearing; Tatu Hatem rose to become Brazil's most fearsome catch-based practitioner, only becoming widely recognized long after he proved the art's effectiveness.

Their stories aren't obscured by brand names or weight-class supremacy—they're defined by **submissions that proved catch's utility without need for ceremony**. Their victories against Gracies and giants are surviving imprints—strong, silent markers of catch wrestling's depth.

Catch's hooks never loosen. They still hold on—in every no-gi scramble, every ride-and-submit transition, every wrist crank that snaps shut. Rufino, Tatu—they stood on both ends of catch wrestling's Brazilian journey, and their legacy endures. History may have overlooked them—but this book ensures they won't be forgotten.

Chapter 17:

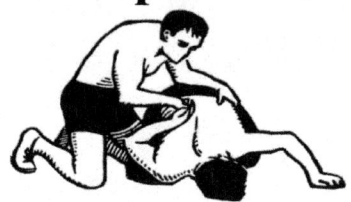

Catch Roots in Western Canada

While Wigan, England is often named the spiritual home of catch wrestling, Western Canada—rugged, cold, and working-class—offered the perfect parallel. Calgary in the mid-20th century was still a city of cowboys and industrial grit. There were no gleaming dojos. Wrestling was an honest trade. And Stu Hart understood that better than most.

Catch wrestling arrived on Canadian soil through itinerant shooters, Commonwealth-era carnival circuits, and early grappling immigrants. It simmered quietly until Hart crystallized it into something living. He took that raw, unforgiving style and forged it into a system—not just of technique, but of toughness.

How Stu Hart Shaped the Style

What made Hart's system uniquely Canadian was its grim practicality. He emphasized:

- **Cross-body pressure** as a primary control method
- **Leg rides** with integrated pin and crank transitions
- **"Wrist control as posture control"** —breaking a man's base at the elbow, not the hip

- **Crossface and neck leverage**—to force reactions and open space
- **Ride-to-crank chains** designed to break not bones, but will

Hart saw wrestling as combat preparation, not choreography. He didn't reject showmanship—but it came *after* you learned how to really hook someone.

Even Bret Hart once said, *"When my dad locked something on you, it wasn't just to show you—it was to convince your nervous system."*

Dungeon Drills: Sample Session Breakdown

From oral accounts and family recollections, here's a composite Dungeon-style training session:

Warm-Up (20–30 min):

- Hindu squats and pushups
- Mat slaps and neck bridging
- Shrimping and tight circle sprawls

Technical Emphasis (30–40 min):

- Double wrist lock from waist ride

- Spiral ride to bar-arm crank
- Cradle series with pressure-based finishes
- Toe hold entries from crossbody pin

Live Rounds (30 min):

- Positional sparring from mount and front headlock
- Escape-only rounds: get out or be stretched
- "Quiet rolling" — Stu's favorite: roll, no coaching, no talking—just feel

Final Stretch (literally):

- Stu applies a submission or stretch to each wrestler while correcting their form, breathing, or posture—part technique, part rite of passage.

Behind Closed Doors: Real Hookers in a Worker's World

Stu was one of the few people in pro wrestling who maintained a hidden cadre of true shooters—men who knew how to protect the business by stretching anyone who got out of line. "Hookers," as they were called, were deployed backstage or quietly challenged visiting talent whose egos outweighed their ability.

In Calgary, this wasn't a myth. It was policy.

Stu's Dungeon trained you how to work—but also how to shoot. Just in case.

When Wrestling Left Calgary—but the Grip Remained

Even as WWE swallowed the territories and Stampede Wrestling dissolved, the Dungeon's aura remained. Hart-trained wrestlers carried his submission-heavy, control-based grappling across the globe.

You can see its fingerprints on:

- **Bret Hart's sharpshooter**: A stylized toe hold
- **Chris Benoit's crossface**: Right out of Wigan's pain catalog
- **Ken Shamrock's neck-and-arm rides in Pancrase**
- **Natalya Neidhart and Tyson Kidd's chain wrestling** on modern TV cards

A Legacy Etched in Silence

The Dungeon didn't brag. It didn't advertise. It didn't even have a sign. But those who went through it carried the bruises—and the benefits—for life.

When they entered other gyms, their body language gave them away: tight posture, heavy hips, quiet confidence. They didn't talk about what they'd learned. They showed it, usually with a tight ride, a crank they never had to finish, or a look that said, "I've felt worse under the house."

The Dungeon wasn't just a place.

It was a crucible.

A whisper wrapped in concrete.

A prayer answered in pressure.

And if you ever trained there, you didn't leave with a certificate.

You left with a hook in your soul.

Chapter 18:

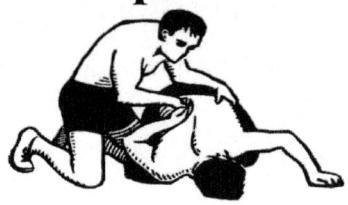

Llaveo y Lucha – Catch Wrestling's Hidden Roots in Mexican Lucha Libre

When the average fan watches lucha libre—the vibrant, high-flying, mask-wearing form of Mexican professional wrestling—they see theater. Acrobatics. Lightning-fast movement. But beneath the aerial antics lies a quiet, gripping foundation. One forged not in flight, but in control. In leverage. In pain. At the base of lucha libre's stylistic tree is a thick, coiled root: catch-as-catch-can wrestling.

This chapter peels back the layers of capes and crowdwork to reveal how catch wrestling helped shape lucha's earliest evolution—and how its submission-based DNA still pulses through Mexico's most flamboyant art form.

Before the Masks: How Catch Wrestling Entered Mexico

At the dawn of the 20th century, before "El Santo" ever donned silver or arenas filled with chants, Mexico was already wrestling. Traveling grapplers from Europe and the United States brought Greco-Roman and catch wrestling through sporting exhibitions, carnivals, and immigrant communities. These weren't choreographed shows—they were real contests of pain and pride.

Many of these early catch wrestlers settled in Mexico or traveled on circuits that touched cities like Mexico City, Monterrey, and Guadalajara. Their mat style—pin-focused, submission-savvy, and full of folk style flair—quickly found an audience and began influencing local fighters who had never worn a gi and never heard of jiu-jitsu.

The Silent Founders: Enrique Ugartechea and Early Hybrids

Mexico's first native-born wrestling icon, **Enrique Ugartechea**, developed a hybrid grappling system in the early 1900s that blended Mexican street fighting with techniques from Greco-Roman and American-style catch. While his name rarely makes it onto modern lucha libre banners, he laid the groundwork for a generation of fighters who would use *llaveo*—the Mexican term for submission chaining—as their core grappling language.

These weren't just holds for show. They were drawn from catch wrestling's ride-to-finish logic. The snap of a front headlock. The torque of a double wrist lock. These "llaves," or keys, weren't entries into drama—they were entries into agony.

The Birth of Lucha Libre—and What Stayed on the Mat

When **Salvador Lutteroth** founded Empresa Mexicana de Lucha Libre (EMLL) in 1933, he wanted to build a national spectacle. He brought in American wrestlers to help populate early cards—many of whom had catch wrestling training from U.S. circuits.

At the same time, Mexican fighters developed their own distinct style: agile, theatrical, but still rooted in submissions. Lucha libre embraced acrobatics—but never discarded *llaveo y contra-llaveo* (hold and counterhold), the mat-based chess that catch wrestling perfected.

Early stars like **El Médico Asesino**, **Gory Guerrero**, and **Black Shadow** were masters of submission flow. They didn't learn from judo academies or jiu-jitsu schools. Their "llaves" came from traveling hookers and local catch holdovers. Wrist traps, toe holds, step-over cranks, banana splits—all elements seen in both catch and early lucha.

A Mat Style in a Masked World

Even as lucha libre became more theatrical in the postwar years—with high spots, elaborate personas, and movie stardom for legends like El Santo and Blue Demon—the style retained its grounded roots. Mexican wrestling schools, especially traditional ones like **Gimnasio Olímpico**, taught submission chains before teaching top-rope dives.

Students drilled:

- Waist control to arm lock transitions
- Double wrist lock (kimura) chains from various rides
- Leg entanglements leading to toe holds and banana splits
- Pin-to-submission transitions, classic catch staples

Many of these training sequences would look more at home in Wigan or Iowa than in a lucha ring—but they laid the platform for every flying headscissors that came after.

Lucha Libre's Unspoken Catch Legacy

While Mexican grappling never branded itself "catch wrestling," its practice echoed the same philosophy:

- *Finish fast, flow faster*
- *Submission over showboating—until the show starts*
- *Pain taught silently, through repetition and ride*

The great irony is that many of Mexico's most elegant performers were born in pain-based training halls. Their holds weren't borrowed from jiu-jitsu. They were inherited from anonymous hookers, local catchmen, and hybrid teachers who never chased glory—only grip.

Catch's Echo in Modern Mexican MMA

Today, as Mexico produces a new wave of elite MMA athletes, catch's influence emerges again. Fighters like **Yair Rodríguez** and **Brandon Moreno** may not call themselves catch wrestlers, but their ground control and top pressure often reflect the same principles taught in lucha gyms decades ago.

Meanwhile, some lucha libre schools, like **Gym "Memo" Diaz** and **Baja Grappling Club,** have openly reintroduced classic pin-and-crank drills, bringing the loop full circle.

Catch wrestling didn't just pass through Mexico. It rooted itself in the mat, slipped on a mask, and flew.

But its hooks are still there. Under every arm drag. Behind every   hold.
In every "llave" that leaves an opponent gasping, asking themselves what just happened.

That, amigo, was catch.

Chapter 19:

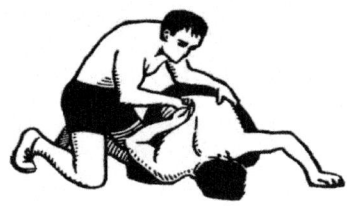

When Real Shooters Enter the Spotlight

In the glimmering world of modern pro wrestling—where fireworks explode, cameras swirl, and characters clash like comic book titans—there's still a special breed of athlete who carries a different kind of weight to the ring. Not the weight of spectacle, but the quiet tension of possibility. The unspoken knowledge that, if pushed, they could turn the match real.

These are today's catch-influenced wrestlers. Shooters in the age of storyline. Grapplers who don't just perform holds—they apply them with the kind of precision that gives locker rooms pause and fans goosebumps. This chapter is about the bridge between hook and hype, where technique meets television and catch wrestling lingers beneath the lights.

The Shooter's Aura in the Modern Era

Backstage, it's called "having the rep." Being the guy (or woman) that people know can go—if they ever need to. In an era defined by choreography and cooperation, being a shooter means carrying a different kind of gravity.

You don't have to announce it. You just have to float, ride, grip, and crank differently. And fans feel it—even if they can't name it.

The Key Players: Catch in Today's Big Leagues

Timothy Thatcher

A throwback with cauliflower ears and a pain-first style, Thatcher built a cult following through his catch-influenced grappling. His matches—especially in EVOLVE, PROGRESS, and NXT—feel like grimy, intimate struggles. Wrist control, crossface pressure, relentless riding. He doesn't "do moves." He imposes holds.

Minoru Suzuki

Revered in Japan and abroad, Suzuki is a veteran of UWF, Pancrase, and NJPW, blending stiff strikes with shoot-style grappling. A student of Fujiwara (and by lineage, Karl Gotch), his matches are catch chess with punches. The way he floats into cranks? That's Wigan.

Zack Sabre Jr.

The British technician fuses World of Sport fluidity with submission chaining straight from a catch syllabus. He transitions from arm locks to neck traps with eerie calm, often winning matches with holds you didn't see coming— until they were too late. His style is grace with venom.

Josh Barnett

While rarely under the bright lights of weekly wrestling TV, Barnett's *Bloodsport* events reintroduced fans to wrestling as legitimate combat. He's arguably the most visible modern ambassador of catch in the U.S., a former UFC champ who cranks double wrist locks like they're gospel.

Daniel Garcia

A rising name in AEW, Garcia blends amateur wrestling with BJJ and catch-style mat work. He favors smothering top control and submission pressure—more shooter than showman, but with enough personality to sell both.

Bloodsport, Shoot-Style Revivals & Catch's New Platforms

The *Josh Barnett's Bloodsport* series—modeled after early Pancrase and UWFI—has become a proving ground for modern shooter aesthetics. No ropes. No pins. Knockout or tap only. The format is pure hooker homage, and wrestlers like Davey Boy Smith Jr., Erik Hammer, and Jon Moxley have embraced the environment.

Other independent promotions—like *GCW's Fight Club*, *GLEAT* in Japan, and UK's *Catch Wrestling World Grand Prix*—also feature strong style fusion, showcasing the enduring appeal of catch-influenced storytelling in wrestling.

When the Hook Comes Out: Real Moments in Fake Matches

Every once in a while, the shoot shows up. Someone stiffens up. Someone forgets the plan. And the "catch guy" turns it down just enough to remind them: this can be real whenever we need it to be.

Those moments—where the transition isn't smooth, but suffocating—are love letters to catch wrestling. Invisible to most, undeniable to those who know.

Catch isn't always announced on the marquee. But when the hold tightens, when the crowd gets quiet, and when the wrestler on top *leans in just enough*—you know it's there.

Hooks behind the hype.
Control behind the cape.

And in the spotlight, they shine a little differently. Because they can end it… if they want to.

Chapter 20:

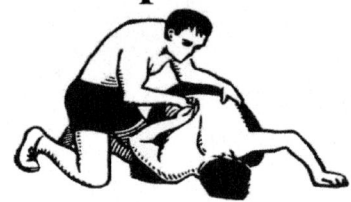

Catch wrestling has always been more than just another grappling style—it's an attitude. A philosophy of domination through leverage, pressure, and pain. While many submission arts focus on patience and positions, catch-as-catch-can charges forward with relentless control and brutal intent. Its techniques aren't beautiful in the classical sense; they're efficient, suffocating, and unforgiving. Where jiu-jitsu plays chess, catch plays poker—with a knife under the table. To understand catch, one doesn't just need to study its techniques but feel the grind of the ride, the crank of the hook, the breathless panic under pressure. This chapter explores what makes catch wrestling distinct and why its signature techniques leave such an indelible impression on anyone who's ever rolled with a true hooker.

The most iconic component of catch wrestling is its submission arsenal—referred to not just as holds, but as "hooks." In catch vernacular, a hook isn't just a way to make someone tap; it's a way to make them *quit*. It's a submission meant to finish a fight, not delay it. The double wrist lock, for instance—known more widely as the kimura—is a cornerstone of catch wrestling, favored because it can be applied from almost any position. Top ride, bottom scramble, standing clinch—anywhere you can get two hands on a wrist and elbow, you can finish the match. But in catch, it's not about securing control and then slowly isolating an arm. The wrist lock is a weapon that appears mid-transition, hiding behind movement, catching the opponent when they least expect it.

Then there's the toe hold—brutal, efficient, and often misunderstood. Unlike modern no-gi systems that obsess over heel hooks, catch favors the straight toe hold: twisted with maximum torque from a leg ride or cross-body control. Catch toe holds aren't isolated threats—they're chained from scrambles and pinned positions, often combined with back pressure or hip traps to force an opponent into pure survival mode. Other classic hooks include the neck crank, banana split, crotch cradle, and face lock—all designed to bend the opponent's body in directions it was never meant to go. There's a reason old catch guys wore expressions like stone: they weren't playing. They were grinding.

What truly sets catch wrestling apart, however, isn't just its submissions—it's how the fight gets there. Catch prioritizes *riding pressure*—the art of sticking to an opponent like glue and draining their will to escape. The ride is the grind. It's not just being on top; it's weaponizing top position. A skilled catch wrestler doesn't need flashy movement. They simply float, adjust weight subtly, and shut down every escape.

Waist rides, spiral rides, leg rides—all tools to trap hips, control posture, and open submission windows. Unlike some styles that prefer to reset during transitions or scramble for reversals, catch wrestlers prefer to smother, pin, and crank from wherever they land.

Leg rides, in particular, are a catch staple. Hooking a leg, stretching the groin, and transitioning into toe holds or banana splits creates a nasty mixture of pain and control. While BJJ teaches positional security before submissions, catch teaches simultaneous attack and control. Cradle positions—both far-side and near-side—become launch points for splits, tilts, and joint locks. The chain is everything. If one submission doesn't land, the ride doesn't stop. It rolls into the next one, applying constant pressure like waves breaking on the shore.

In catch, control precedes everything. Not in the jiu-jitsu sense of gradually advancing position, but in the suffocating, limb-isolating, breath-stealing way that makes every escape feel like a mistake. That philosophy is why catch chains its submissions so aggressively. There is no "achieve mount, then secure an armbar." Instead, a catch wrestler might threaten a bar arm, bait a reaction, slide into a crossface crank, then finish with a toe hold—all within seconds. It's not clean. It's not always pretty. But it's always effective.

One of the most misunderstood elements of catch wrestling is its use of pins—not as a way to score, but as a weapon. In modern submission grappling, pins are often seen as rest positions. In catch, they're offensive platforms. A side headlock pin isn't just control—it's a grind that sets up neck cranks. A crossbody pin becomes a trap for a step-over toe hold. Pins are punishment, not pause. That's the difference. You don't pin someone to wait. You pin them so they want out—and when they reach, you hook.

Even the transitions in catch tell a story of intent. There's no scramble for the sake of movement. Every shift in pressure has a purpose. Float to mount? It's to crank the head. Shift to the waist ride? You're hunting the far-side arm. Everything is done with the goal of breaking—not just balance, but resolve. Catch isn't a style that lets you breathe. That's by design.

And then there's the swagger. Catch wrestlers don't just apply technique. They impose it. There's a mentality that comes with grinding someone into the mat—not with speed or explosions, but with steady pressure and refusal to relent.

It's not uncommon for someone new to the style to feel as if they're drowning without ever being submitted. That's catch. It teaches you what it's like to lose before the finish even comes.

Because above all else, catch wrestling is about dominance. The double wrist lock doesn't whisper—it wrenches. The toe hold doesn't ask—it takes. The ride doesn't suggest—it insists. You don't win in catch by outscoring someone. You win by *making them want out.*

So if jiu-jitsu is the art of the gentle way, and sambo the art of versatility, then catch wrestling is the art of the *inevitable.* Not flashy. Not fancy. Just tight, mean, and real.

There are no shortcuts in catch. Only sharp turns, tight grips, and the choice to either suffer or submit. And for those who commit to the style, the path is clear: hook hard. Ride harder. Never let them breathe.

Because in catch wrestling, if they can't move, they can't fight. And if they can't fight, you've already won.

Chapter 21:

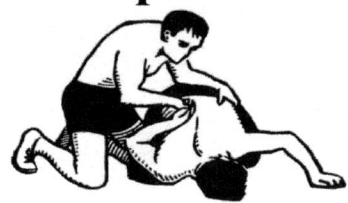

No Gentle Art – The Psychology of the Catch Wrestler

Catch wrestling has never called itself gentle. It isn't spiritual. It doesn't come wrapped in bowing rituals or Latin proverbs. Its central lesson isn't harmony—it's control. And yet, behind every wrist lock, ride, or crank is something deeper than muscle memory. A mindset. A particular way of thinking that turns technique into intent and separates the merely technical from the truly dangerous.

This chapter isn't about what catch wrestlers do. It's about how they think. The psychology of pressure, of presence, of quiet dominance. Because when two grapplers tie up, what decides the match isn't just mechanics—it's who refuses to break. And no one carries that trait quite like the catch wrestler.

Catch was never meant to be fair. It was forged in carnivals, gyms without mats, and locker rooms that didn't welcome outsiders. From the beginning, it taught pain as education and control as conversation. That philosophy shapes everything: the way catch wrestlers train, the way they apply technique, the way they carry themselves on and off the mat. For catch wrestlers, grappling isn't just about winning. It's about proving you *could've ended it* sooner—if you wanted to.

The mindset starts with one word: intent. Catch doesn't wait. It doesn't hunt for ideal scenarios. It creates them. A catch wrestler moves forward not just with pressure, but with the belief that every exchange is an opportunity to finish. And finishing doesn't always mean tapping an opponent—it might mean making them miserable, erasing their confidence, exhausting their breath until the tap is just a formality. This is where catch's psychological power comes from: its practitioners learn to weaponize frustration, panic, and fatigue. They thrive in grind. They don't need the perfect moment—they make the current one unbearable.

Unlike many martial arts that prize calm detachment, catch leans into the confrontation. It teaches its practitioners not to avoid pain, but to build tolerance for it—then return it twice as hard. There's a grim pride in knowing you've suffered worse in training than you'll face in any match. The old Snake Pit mantra—"You don't get good until someone else hurts"—wasn't bravado. It was doctrine.

Catch wrestlers are problem solvers under duress. They don't think in terms of sequences—they think in traps. How to bait an opponent into resisting the wrong way. How to float just high enough to trigger a scramble—then catch the neck when it lifts. Their style is as much psychological warfare as it is physical execution. They thrive on making opponents choose between two bad options: stay still and get crushed, or move and get caught.

Confidence, too, is different in catch wrestling. It's quieter. Not arrogant—but certain. It's what happens when you've been stretched by someone who could have broken you—and you came back. There's no need to show off when you know your technique lives in pain. That quiet certainty creates presence. You feel a catch wrestler's composure before they touch you. And when they do? It's instant control. Not a grip. A grip *and* an intention.

Another key piece of the catch mindset is adaptability. A catch wrestler doesn't rely on rules or structure. Their art was born in matches with no time limit, no points, no resets. They don't need a system—they *are* the system. This makes them ruthless in a scramble and calm in chaos. Their training teaches them to pressure through hesitation and exploit flinches. They don't reset. They redirect.

Control isn't something they take—it's something they *expect* to have. And even when losing, a catch wrestler often looks unfazed. That's not illusion. It's experience. They've rolled for hours in garages, basements, and sweatbox gyms where tapping wasn't frowned upon—but quitting mentally was. They don't just condition their bodies. They condition their mindset to remain dangerous in every position.

There's a myth that catch wrestling is about aggression. But the truth is more nuanced. Catch isn't angry. It's deliberate. There's no wasted movement, no emotional chaos. When a catch wrestler pins you, it feels surgical. Like they've already solved the problem before you knew you had one.

And that's the sharpest weapon a catch wrestler ever carries: awareness. Not just of their opponent's body—but their breathing, their tension, their mental breaks. They don't look for mistakes. They *engineer* them.

So while technique matters, what separates a great catch wrestler from a good one isn't just how tight the toe hold is—it's *when* they apply it. Whether they can smell fatigue. Whether they can press the neck just enough to steal posture, then float to a finish. It's not brute force. It's predatory calculation.

That's why catch wrestling, when done right, leaves a unique impression on those who face it. You don't just lose. You feel *taken apart*. Not quickly—but piece by piece.

Controlled. Examined. Outthought. That kind of experience sticks. And that kind of grappler becomes something more than technical—they become unforgettable.

Because anyone can learn a hold.
Not everyone can become a hooker.

And the ones who do?
They don't just grip with their hands.

They grip with their *mind*—and they don't let go.

Chapter 22:

Whispered Lessons – What Can't Be Written

Catch wrestling is a cruel teacher. It doesn't issue certificates or hand out belts. Its lessons don't come in tidy paragraphs, and its rules rarely make it to ink. Instead, what survives— what travels across decades and continents—isn't curriculum. It's instinct. It's whispers. The half-jokes with teeth. The little phrases muttered before a hold is tightened. The warnings disguised as advice.

These are the teachings that can't be written. And they're what make catch wrestling something more than a style— they make it a lineage of *feel*.

No school of grappling has a sharper sense of mat wisdom than catch. This is a culture where pressure is language and pain is punctuation. What survives from generation to generation isn't a syllabus—it's a scowl, a grip, a pause before the crank. You don't read your way into catch. You suffer your way in. And if you pay attention, the old hookers will tell you what they know. But not all at once. Only when you're ready. And never without testing your patience first.

Here are some of the whispered truths that have stitched themselves into the style:

"Control before you submit. Submit before you hurt. Hurt if you must."

This mantra—attributed to Billy Robinson—sums up the ethics of catch. Submissions in catch are fast, mean, and deliberate. But mastery comes from knowing *when* to hook, not just *how*. A true catch wrestler doesn't abuse technique—they use it to create inevitability.

"If you can't ride, you can't win."

Everything in catch is built on top control. It's not just about staying on top—it's about turning top position into a factory of failure for your opponent. They stand? Return them. They stall? Pin them. They scramble? Float and punish. Hooks are meaningless if you can't stay there long enough to set them.

"A good hold makes them think. A great hold makes them talk. The best hold shuts them up."

Catch submissions are designed to end matches—but also to extract reactions. One of the hallmarks of a seasoned hooker is the ability to make opponents *think* they're safe before locking something in—and once the hold is fully on, there's no time for strategy, only instinct. And sometimes, surrender.

"If they breathe, make it harder. If they move, make them regret it."

Catch's riding culture is as much psychological as it is physical. Squeezing space out of someone's lungs is a form of control. Giving them just enough hope to move—and punishing them when they do—is how catch teaches patience without passivity.

"Let them feel the finish before it comes."

The best catch grapplers don't apply sudden submission—they *threaten* it in stages. They let their opponent stew in discomfort until the brain panics first. Catch teaches that pain isn't just a path to the tap—it's a tool to *steer* the match toward it.

"If you didn't hate the warm-up, it wasn't catch."

Old-school conditioning—Hindu squats, neck bridges, sprawls, pushups—wasn't just about fitness. It was about teaching discomfort as a default state. If you're gassed when the match begins, you were never ready to hook. If your neck can't bridge out of a ride, the wrist lock doesn't matter.

"Catch doesn't care who you are. It cares what you can take."

Titles, lineage, and belts mean nothing on the mat. Catch doesn't respect rank—it respects tolerance. And the mat never lies.

"Float like a safe. Not a butterfly."

Unlike the grace of BJJ's flow or the arc of judo's throw, catch floats heavily. Top pressure isn't passive—it's *predatory*. A proper catch float feels like gravity is choosing sides.

"You don't learn catch until someone shows you why you're wrong."

Books won't teach it. Videos won't hurt you. Only another hooker can point out what your grip missed, why your elbow angle is off, or how your spine's just a little too straight to crank. These things don't go on paper. They get passed down *body to body*.

"You'll know it's real when you try to sleep that night."

Because sometimes the best mat lessons don't register right away. They settle in your neck. Your ribs. The quiet ache behind your shoulder blade that says: "You didn't see it coming. Now you know."

The catch mat has no secrets—just slow revelations. You come back tomorrow sore and smarter, until you too become a voice that whispers, corrects, and cranks a little tighter.

There's no manual. Only memory.
No certificate. Only scars.
And no higher compliment than when the old hooker says, "You're starting to feel heavy."

That's when you know: the whispers heard you.

Chapter 23:

Catch Lives: The Sport's Modern Revival

Once whispered in old-school gyms and passed from coach to student like sacred scrolls, catch wrestling is once again stepping into the light—not just as a lineage, but as a live, breathing sport. In recent years, a global resurgence has transformed catch-as-catch-can from an underground tradition into a growing competitive platform, championed by passionate organizers, seasoned coaches, and hungry athletes seeking a rawer, purer form of grappling.

This chapter explores the modern evolution of catch wrestling as a formalized sport—complete with tournaments, ranking systems, and federations focused on preserving its authenticity while adapting it to today's combat landscape.

The Rules of Engagement: What Modern Catch Looks Like

Today's competitive catch retains many of the art's signature elements—emphasis on pinfalls and submissions, no points for position, and a gritty, continuous pace that rewards aggression and control. Matches are typically won by:

- Pinning an opponent's shoulders for a 3-count

- Securing a legitimate submission (with no gi and often limited grip restrictions)
- Outlasting an opponent in a "no time limit, no point" format in some events

Unlike many submission grappling tournaments, catch wrestling maintains its pin-to-win philosophy, which encourages dynamic movement and risk-taking rather than stalling for position. And while rule sets vary slightly between organizations, the focus remains on pressure, precision, and control.

Major Organizations Carrying the Torch

Catch Wrestling Alliance (CWA)

Based in Los Angeles and founded by Raul Ramirez, CWA has hosted the *Catch Wrestling World Championship*—a landmark tournament that drew catch stylists and cross-trained grapplers from around the world. CWA emphasizes tradition, clear rules, and international outreach.

Scientific Wrestling

Founded by Jake Shannon, this organization has played a pivotal role in preserving and promoting authentic catch-as-catch-can. With seminars, coaching certifications, and events inspired by the teachings of Billy Robinson and Karl Gotch, Scientific Wrestling has become a cornerstone for catch in North America and beyond.

Snake Pit U.S.A.

With direct lineage to the famed Wigan Snake Pit, this organization offers structured certification programs and tournaments grounded in traditional British catch. Snake Pit U.S.A., led by coaches like Joel Bane, promotes authentic techniques while helping athletes cross over into MMA and BJJ with solid grappling fundamentals.

American Hook Wrestling Alliance (AHWA)

A newer platform creating regional tournaments and team-based events, AHWA focuses on athlete development and community growth. It represents one of the more grassroots movements in the current ecosystem.

World Catch Wrestling Federation (WCWF)

WCWF has helped standardize modern competition formats while working to unify gyms and events under a clear banner. It also seeks to reconnect international branches of catch wrestling with shared rules and historical consistency.

Catch Wrestling Japan / Real Japan Pro Wrestling (RJPW)

In Japan, catch has remained tightly woven into both shoot wrestling and MMA. Organizations like RJPW, heavily influenced by the teachings of Karl Gotch, continue to promote competitions that blend showmanship with legitimate catch roots.

Hybrid Competitions and Crossovers

Catch wrestling now sees representation in open grappling tournaments, with athletes competing under submission wrestling or no-gi rulesets while preserving catch's core ethos. Submissions like the double wrist lock, neck cranks, and leg rides have become commonplace in modern mats— even if they're now labeled differently.

Athletes with catch backgrounds are making waves in Brazilian jiu-jitsu tournaments, combat jiu-jitsu, and MMA, proving the versatility and staying power of catch-as-catch-can.

The Road Ahead

Catch wrestling still faces challenges: limited visibility, fragmented rule sets, and lack of centralized funding. But its raw appeal—gritty, honest, and brutally effective— resonates more with every passing year. Today's grapplers crave authenticity, and catch delivers that with no flair, no points, and no quit.

Whether you're a wrestler looking to expand your toolkit, a BJJ practitioner interested in hybrid control, or simply a fan drawn to the sport's heritage, modern catch wrestling is no longer hiding in the shadows. It's back on the mat—hooking, cranking, pinning, and building momentum one hard-earned submission at a time.

Chapter 24:

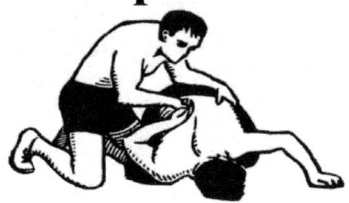

The Eternal Grip

Catch wrestling is the ghost that refuses to disappear. It lurks beneath the surface of every grappling renaissance, every MMA resurgence, every dusty gym where the mat smells like sweat and old ambition. Just when the world forgets it, someone cranks a double wrist lock out of nowhere. Someone floats on top like a safe, not a butterfly. Someone rides through chaos and makes pain look like punctuation. And suddenly, we remember—*oh yes, this still exists.*

Catch was never meant to be preserved in glass. It was born without a flag or a founder, shaped by carnival hookers, coal country grapplers, silent shooters, and mat scientists who didn't care for belts or ceremony. It passed from one bruised body to another, by whispers, by pressure, by wrists that bent the wrong way and voices that said, "Again." It wasn't created to win tournaments. It was designed to *end things.* Quickly, brutally, elegantly.

And yet it survives not because of nostalgia—but because it works. In a world that constantly reinvents fighting, catch doesn't beg for relevance. It lets others come back to it. Legions of young grapplers now explore no-gi, float pressure, and pin-to-hook chaining and discover, to their surprise, that the "new" thing they're learning feels *old*. That's because it is. Whether they call it submission wrestling, hybrid grappling, or control-based no-gi, they're speaking catch in a different accent.

But legacy is never tidy. The story of catch is scarred by politics, buried lineages, fractured federations, and quiet heroes who died before anyone listened. It's a style held together not by institutions, but by sweat, spite, and stubbornness. And that's exactly why it lives.

It lives in the old man at the edge of the mat, correcting your grip with a knuckle. In the student who drills pressure rounds instead of highlight reels. In the pro wrestler who refuses to treat holds as transitions, and the MMA fighter who doesn't play for points. Catch is legacy carried in fingers and forearms, in the thousand tiny lessons that were *never written down*.

It is pain, preserved with love.
It is control, taught by pressure.
It is history, disguised as a hold.

And it's not going anywhere.

Because the grip—when it's real—is eternal.

Guillermo Díaz is a seasoned personal trainer, boxing aficionado, and passionate writer with a deep love for fitness and sports. Born and raised in his hometown in Mexico, Díaz's connection to boxing began early, and by the time he was 20, he had built an impressive amateur record of 24-3-4. His time in the ring shaped not only his understanding of the sport but also his dedication to physical conditioning and mental resilience.

After his competitive boxing career, Guillermo transitioned into coaching, where he now volunteers as a youth boxing coach, helping young athletes build strength, confidence, and discipline in both the sport and their daily lives. His experience in the gym and his firsthand knowledge of boxing techniques, physical fitness, and the importance of perseverance have led him to become a respected voice in the world of sports and fitness.

Díaz writes extensively on topics related to sports, fitness, and the intersection of mental and physical conditioning. His unique perspective blends his athletic background with a passion for helping others achieve their fitness goals, whether it's through the art of boxing or general physical training. When he's not in the gym or at his writing desk, Guillermo enjoys exploring new fitness trends, staying active, and giving back to his community.

Catch Wrestling: The Original Submission Art

Before Brazilian jiu-jitsu, before mixed martial arts, before belts and brackets—there was catch-as-catch-can. Forged in the sweat-soaked carnivals of the 19th century and sharpened in the smoky fight halls of Lancashire, catch wrestling is the brutal, beautiful ancestor of modern grappling.

This book traces its legacy across continents and centuries— from Frank Gotch to Kazushi Sakuraba, from the mats of the Snake Pit to the underground camps of Luta Livre and the masked mystery of lucha libre. Part history, part philosophy, and part no-nonsense manual, *Catch Wrestling: The Original Submission Art* dives deep into the holds, hooks, and mindset that make catch a method of control—not choreography.

Whether you're a fighter, a fan, or a mat-side historian, this is the grip you didn't see coming.

Because real wrestling never taps out.
It catches. And it holds.

Printed in Dunstable, United Kingdom